# *Alavida*

Copyright © 2024 *Alavida*
*Alavida Publishing*

All rights reserved. No portion of this book may be reproduced, stored in a retrieval system, or transmitted in any form or buy any means - electronic, mechanical, photocopy, recording, scanning, or other, with the prior written permission of the author or publisher.
For inquires or requests, please contact the author at:
al@alavidapublishing.com

ISBN: 978-1-959602-37-8

# MYSTICISM UNVEILED

## Exploring the Spiritual Wisdom of the Ages

*Alavida*

This Book is Dedicated to the People
all over the World

# Contents

**Introduction** ............................................... 1
Unveiling Mysticism
Exploring the Spiritual Wisdom of the Ages

**Chapter 1: Advaita Vedanta: Hindu Mysticism ..... 5**

Section 1. Historical Background
Section 2. Key Teachings
Section 3. Practices
Section 4. Influential Figures
Section 5. Sacred Texts

**Chapter 2: Buddhist Mysticism ........................ 17**

Section 1. Vajrayana Path
Section 2. Core Practices
Section 3. Philosophical Concepts
Section 4. Historical Masters
Section 5. The Tibetan Book of the Dead

**Chapter 3: Kabbalah: Jewish Mysticism .............. 31**

Section 1. Origins and Evolution
Section 2. Symbolism and Concepts
Section 3. Mystical Texts
Section 4. Practical Kabbalah
Section 5. Meditation and Gematria

**Chapter 4: Christian Mysticism ........................ 41**

Section 1. Early Mystics
Section 2. Key Practices
Section 3. Prominent Figures
Section 4. Mystical Texts
Section 5. Themes of Union with God

**Chapter 5: Sufism: The Islamic Mystical Path ........ 55**

Section 1. Sufi Origins
Section 2. Spiritual Practices
Section 3. Sufi Orders
Section 4. Notable Sufis
Section 5. Concepts of Fana and Baqa

**Chapter 6: Taoist Mysticism** .............................. 69

Section 1. Foundational Texts
Section 2. Taoist Concepts
Section 3. Alchemy and Immortality
Section 4. Philosophical vs. Religious Taoism
Section 5. Yin and Yang Balance

**Chapter 7: Gnostic Mysticism** ........................... 83

Section 1. Gnostic Beliefs
Section 2. Historical Context
Section 3. Key Texts
Section 4. Influence and Legacy
Section 5. Gnosticism's Modern Relevance

**Chapter 8: Lesser-Known Traditional Mysticism** .... 97

Section 1. Shamanism
Section 2: The Mysticism of Indigenous African Religions
Section 3: Australian Aboriginal Dreamtime
Section 4: Bon: Pre-Buddhist Mysticism of Tibet
Section 5: Alchemical Traditions
Section 6: The Mystical Aspect of Philosophical Taoism
Section 7: Sikh Mysticism

**Conclusion** ......................................................... 107
Integrating Wisdom
The Universal Quest

**Glossary of Terms** .............................................. 113
**Further Reading** ................................................. 115

**Mysticism Unveiled:
Exploring the Spiritual Wisdom of the Ages**

# Introduction

## Unveiling Mysticism

In a world dominated by technology, material pursuits, and the relentless pace of modern life, many of us feel a deep yearning for something more—a connection that transcends the ordinary and touches the profound mysteries of existence. Mysticism, often misunderstood and shrouded in mystery, offers a path to that connection. It invites us to explore the sacred directly, to step beyond the boundaries of intellect and doctrine, and to experience the divine in a way that is deeply personal and transformative.

Imagine standing at the threshold of an ancient temple, its doors slightly ajar. The air around you is thick with anticipation, as if the very stones are whispering secrets from ages past. The space within is not fully revealed, but the glimpse you catch hints at something extraordinary, something beyond the grasp of ordinary perception. This book, *Mysticism Unveiled: Exploring the Spiritual Wisdom of the Ages,* is an invitation to step through those doors. It's an invitation to embark on a journey into the mystical traditions that have shaped human consciousness for millennia.

At its core, mysticism is about direct experience—a personal encounter with the divine that transcends the limitations of language, culture, and time. This universal quest has manifested in various forms across the globe, from the non-dual awareness of Hindu yogis and the contemplative silence of Christian monks to the ecstatic dances of Sufi mystics and the deep stillness of Buddhist meditation. Despite the diversity of these traditions, they all share a common thread: the belief that the boundaries we perceive between self and other, matter and spirit, life and death are mere illusions. To the mystic, these boundaries dissolve, revealing a reality that is whole, unified, and infused with divine presence.

## Exploring the Spiritual Wisdom of the Ages

In the pages that follow, we will journey through the mystical traditions of different cultures, uncovering the wisdom they offer for our own spiritual paths. We will explore how these traditions, while diverse in expression, resonate with common themes of transformation, balance, and the pursuit of deeper understanding. Through the stories of mystics who have walked these paths before us, we will see how their experiences can inspire and guide our own.

But mysticism is not just a relic of the past; it is a living, breathing force that continues to guide and inspire those who seek it. In an age where the external world often overshadows the inner life, the wisdom of the mystics offers a vital counterbalance. It teaches us to look within, to cultivate an awareness of the divine presence in all things, and to develop a deeper connection with ourselves, others, and the universe.

This book is not only for those who identify as spiritual seekers or religious adherents. It is for anyone who has ever felt a sense of wonder or curiosity about the nature of reality, who has questioned the purpose of life, or who has sought answers to profound questions that science and logic alone cannot fully address. As we delve into the mystical paths of Advaita Vedanta, Buddhism, Kabbalah, Christian mysticism, Sufism, Taoism, and Gnosticism, as well as some lesser-known traditional mysticism, we will uncover the universal truths that lie at the heart of these traditions.

As we embark on this journey together, let us remember that the wisdom of the ages is not just something to be admired from afar. It is a living force, inviting us to awaken to the reality that lies beyond the confines of ordinary perception. Mysticism is not about escaping the world but engaging with it more deeply, discovering that the divine has always been within us, waiting to be unveiled.

**Advaita Vedanta: Hindu Mysticism**

# Chapter 1: Advaita Vedanta: Hindu Mysticism

## Section 1. Historical Background

The roots of Advaita Vedanta, one of the most profound and influential schools of Hindu philosophy, stretch back over two millennia, deep into the spiritual heart of ancient India. To understand Advaita Vedanta is to journey back to a time when sages and seekers wandered the forests and riverbanks, absorbed in the quest for ultimate truth. These ancient sages, the Rishis, composed the Upanishads—texts that form the philosophical core of Hinduism and the foundation of Advaita Vedanta.

Imagine yourself in the dense forests of the Indian subcontinent, where the air is thick with the scent of earth and the sounds of nature form a serene backdrop. Here, under the canopy of ancient trees, the Rishis sat in deep meditation, seeking to unravel the mysteries of existence. Their insights, captured in the Upanishads, speak of a reality that transcends the physical world, a reality that is at once infinite and intimately connected to the self.

The word "Advaita" means "non-dual," and this simple yet profound concept is at the heart of the philosophy. What it really states is that there is no fundamental separation between the self (Atman) and the ultimate reality (Brahman). This idea was revolutionary in a time when various schools of thought debated the nature of the self, the universe, and the divine. The Upanishads declared, in no uncertain terms, that the essence of the individual and the cosmos is one and the same—a single, unified reality.

But it wasn't until the 8th century CE that Advaita Vedanta was fully systematized by one of India's greatest philosophers, Adi Shankaracharya. Born in a small village in Kerala, Shankaracharya was a prodigy who, by the age of eight, had mastered the Vedas and set out on a journey that would forever change the landscape of Indian philosophy. Shankaracharya traveled the length and breadth of India, engaging in debates with scholars of other schools of thought, establishing monastic centers (mathas), and composing extensive commentaries on the Upanishads, the Bhagavad Gita, and the Brahma Sutras.

Through his teachings, Shankaracharya emphasized the illusory nature of the world, known as Maya, and the importance of realizing the non-dual nature of Atman and Brahman. He argued that ignorance (Avidya) of this fundamental truth is the root cause of all suffering, and that liberation (Moksha) could only be attained through self-realization and the knowledge of non-duality.

The historical context of Shankaracharya's life is as important as the philosophy he propagated. During his time, India was a land of immense religious and philosophical diversity, with numerous sects and schools vying for prominence. Shankaracharya's genius lay not only in his philosophical acumen but also in his ability to unify and reconcile various strands of Hindu thought under the banner of Advaita Vedanta. His establishment of four monastic orders in the cardinal directions of India ensured the survival and propagation of his teachings, which continue to flourish to this day.

Shankaracharya's influence extended far beyond the philosophical sphere; he played a crucial role in revitalizing Hinduism at a time when it was threatened by both internal divisions and external challenges. His life and work are celebrated in numerous hagiographies, where he is often portrayed as a divine incarnation, sent to restore the true knowledge of the self and the universe.

As we delve into the teachings of Advaita Vedanta, it's important to keep in mind this rich historical backdrop—put together by the insights of ancient sages and the genius of Shankaracharya. The philosophy that emerged from this confluence is not just a set of abstract ideas but a living tradition that has guided countless seekers on their journey toward self-realization.

## Section 2. Key Teachings

At the heart of Advaita Vedanta lies a set of teachings that challenge our everyday perceptions and invite us to explore the deeper truths of existence. These teachings, though profound and subtle, are accessible to anyone willing to look beyond the surface of life and into the nature of reality itself.

The most fundamental teaching of Advaita Vedanta is the concept of non-duality, or *Advaita*. This principle asserts that there is no real separation between the self (*Atman*) and the ultimate reality (*Brahman*). In our everyday experience, we perceive ourselves as distinct individuals, separate from the world around us. However, Advaita Vedanta teaches that this sense of separateness is an illusion—*Maya*—created by our ignorance of the true nature of reality. In truth, *Atman* and *Brahman* are one and the same, and to realize this oneness is to attain liberation (*Moksha*).

Consider the analogy of a wave in the ocean. From a distance, we see individual waves rising and falling, each with its own shape and form. But upon closer inspection, we realize that each wave is nothing more than the ocean itself, momentarily appearing as something distinct. In the same way, our individual selves are like waves in the ocean of *Brahman*—temporary expressions of a singular, infinite reality.

Another key teaching of Advaita Vedanta is the doctrine of *Maya*, the cosmic illusion that causes us to perceive the world as composed of separate entities. *Maya* is not merely an illusion in the sense of being false or unreal; rather, it is a misperception of the underlying reality. The world, as we experience it, is not inherently separate from *Brahman*, but our limited understanding causes us to see it as such. The purpose of spiritual practice in Advaita Vedanta is to pierce through this veil of *Maya* and perceive the true, undivided nature of reality.

Central to this process of awakening is the practice of *Jnana Yoga*, the path of knowledge. Unlike other forms of yoga, which may focus on physical postures or devotional practices, *Jnana Yoga* involves deep inquiry into the nature of the self and the universe. It is a contemplative path that encourages seekers to ask fundamental questions: Who am I? What is the nature of the world? What is the ultimate reality? Through this process of inquiry, the seeker gradually sheds layers of ignorance and moves closer to the realization of non-duality.

A key practice within *Jnana Yoga* is *Neti Neti*, a method of self-inquiry that involves the systematic negation of all that is not the true self. The phrase *Neti Neti* means "not this, not that," and it reflects the process of discerning what is real from what is illusory. By rejecting identification with the body, mind, and emotions—each of which is transient and subject to change—the seeker arrives at the realization that the true self, *Atman*, is beyond all dualities, beyond all categories of thought and perception.

Advaita Vedanta also teaches the importance of a Guru, or spiritual teacher, in guiding the seeker toward self-realization. The Guru is seen as a living embodiment of *Brahman*, and their role is to impart the teachings, clarify doubts, and help the disciple navigate the challenges of the spiritual path. The relationship between Guru and disciple is considered sacred, with the Guru often regarded as a manifestation of the divine.

Finally, the goal of Advaita Vedanta is not simply intellectual understanding but the direct, experiential realization of non-duality. This realization, often described as a state of pure consciousness or *Turiya*, is beyond the mind and senses. It is a state of being in which the seeker transcends all dualities and recognizes the self as identical with *Brahman* —infinite, eternal, and blissful.

The key teachings of Advaita Vedanta offer a path to understanding the deepest truths of existence. They challenge us to look beyond the apparent separateness of the world and realize the underlying unity of all life. Through study, contemplation, and the guidance of a Guru, these teachings can lead to the ultimate realization of non-duality, freeing us from the cycle of birth and death and opening the door to a life of profound peace and fulfillment.

### Section 3. Practices

The practices of Advaita Vedanta are designed to help individuals realize their true nature and experience the oneness that lies at the heart of existence. These practices are not about rituals or outward displays of devotion but are focused on inner transformation and self-realization.

One of the most fundamental practices in Advaita Vedanta is self-inquiry, often referred to as *Vichara*. This involves a deep, continuous questioning of one's own identity with the central question, "Who am I?" The purpose of this practice is to peel away the layers of false identification—our body, mind, emotions, and ego—until we uncover the true self, which is beyond all these layers. The idea is to move past the superficial aspects of who we think we are and reach the essence of our being, which is the same as the essence of the universe.

Another important practice is meditation. In Advaita Vedanta, meditation is not about focusing on an object or a thought but about resting in the awareness of the self. This practice is often described as "just being"—allowing thoughts and sensations to come and go without attachment, while remaining centered in the experience of pure consciousness. Through regular meditation, practitioners can experience moments of non-duality, where the distinction between self and other fades away, revealing the underlying unity of all existence.

Discrimination and detachment are also key practices in Advaita Vedanta. Discrimination, known as *Viveka*, involves the ability to distinguish between what is real and what is not, between the eternal and the temporary. Practitioners are encouraged to constantly reflect on the nature of reality, recognizing that the material world is transient and ever-changing, while the true self is eternal and unchanging. Detachment, or *Vairagya*, complements this by encouraging individuals to let go of attachments to material possessions, desires, and even personal ambitions. By cultivating detachment, practitioners can free themselves from the distractions of the world and focus on realizing their true nature.

The study of scriptures is another vital practice. Advaita Vedanta draws heavily on the teachings of the Upanishads, the Bhagavad Gita, and the Brahma Sutras. By studying these texts, practitioners gain insight into the nature of reality and the path to self-realization. However, this study is not merely academic; it is meant to be a contemplative practice where the teachings are deeply internalized and reflected upon, leading to direct personal experience.

Finally, Satsang, or the company of the wise, plays a significant role in the practice of Advaita Vedanta. Engaging with a Guru or a community of like-minded seekers provides support, guidance, and inspiration on the spiritual path. The presence of a Guru is particularly important, as the Guru is seen as a living embodiment of the truth that the seeker is trying to realize. Through dialogue, reflection, and shared practice, Satsang helps to reinforce the teachings and keeps the practitioner focused on their goal.

These practices, when followed with dedication and sincerity, guide the practitioner toward the ultimate realization that their true self is not separate from the infinite reality of Brahman. This realization brings about a profound inner transformation, leading to a state of lasting peace, freedom, and unity with all existence.

### Section 4. Influential Figures

Advaita Vedanta has been shaped and enriched by numerous influential figures, each of whom has played a significant role in preserving and propagating its teachings.

**Adi Shankaracharya** is perhaps the most revered figure in the Advaita tradition. Born in the 8th century CE, Shankaracharya is credited with reviving and systematizing Advaita Vedanta, making it one of the most important schools of Hindu philosophy. His commentaries on the Upanishads, the Bhagavad Gita, and the Brahma Sutras are considered foundational texts in the tradition. Shankaracharya's teachings emphasize the non-dual nature of reality, asserting that the individual self (Atman) is identical to the ultimate reality (Brahman). He established monastic centers across India to ensure the continued study and practice of Advaita Vedanta, and his influence is still felt today in the spiritual landscape of Hinduism.

**Ramana Maharshi** is a modern-day sage who brought the teachings of Advaita Vedanta to a global audience. Born in 1879 in Tamil Nadu, India, Ramana Maharshi experienced a profound spiritual awakening at the age of 16, leading him to realize the non-dual nature of existence. He spent most of his life at the Arunachala mountain, where he guided seekers through the practice of self-inquiry. Ramana Maharshi's teachings are characterized by their simplicity and directness, focusing on the question, "Who am I?" His approach has inspired countless people around the world to explore the depths of their own consciousness.

**Swami Vivekananda**, a disciple of the mystic Ramakrishna, also played a crucial role in bringing Advaita Vedanta to the West. His famous address at the Parliament of the World's Religions in Chicago in 1893 introduced the concepts of Advaita Vedanta to a global audience, emphasizing the unity of all religions and the divinity inherent in every individual. Vivekananda's teachings highlighted the practical application of Advaita Vedanta, encouraging people to realize their true nature and to live in harmony with the world around them.

**Nisargadatta Maharaj** is another influential figure in the modern Advaita tradition. A self-realized master from Mumbai, India, Nisargadatta's teachings focus on the direct experience of non-duality. His book, *I Am That*, is considered a classic in Advaita literature, offering clear and uncompromising guidance on realizing one's true nature. Nisargadatta's approach is straightforward, emphasizing the importance of self-inquiry and the direct experience of the truth beyond concepts and ideas.

These influential figures have each contributed to the rich tapestry of Advaita Vedanta, ensuring its relevance and accessibility for spiritual seekers across generations. Their teachings continue to inspire and guide those on the path to self-realization, offering a timeless message of unity, freedom, and inner peace.

**Section 5. Sacred Texts**

The sacred texts of Advaita Vedanta provide the philosophical and spiritual foundation for its teachings. These texts are revered not just as scripture but as living guides for those on the path to self-realization.

The **Upanishads** are among the most important texts in Advaita Vedanta. Often referred to as the Vedanta, meaning the culmination of the Vedas, the Upanishads explore the nature of reality, the self (Atman), and the ultimate reality (Brahman). These ancient scriptures delve into profound philosophical questions, offering insights into the non-dual nature of existence. The Mahavakyas, or great sayings found in the Upanishads, such as "Tat Tvam Asi"

(Thou Art That), encapsulate the essence of Advaita Vedanta's teachings.

The **Bhagavad Gita** is another key text in Advaita Vedanta. While it is revered across various schools of Hindu philosophy, the Gita's teachings on the nature of the self and the unity of all existence resonate deeply with Advaita Vedanta. In his commentary on the Bhagavad Gita, Adi Shankaracharya emphasizes the non-dual teachings, highlighting the identity of the individual soul (Atman) with Brahman. The Gita's discourse on karma, yoga, and self-knowledge serves as a practical guide for spiritual seekers.

The **Brahma Sutras** systematically organize and interpret the teachings of the Upanishads, providing a coherent framework for Advaita Vedanta. Adi Shankaracharya's commentary on the Brahma Sutras is a foundational text in the tradition, offering insights into the nature of reality, the means of knowledge, and the path to liberation. The Brahma Sutras address various philosophical questions and objections, defending the non-dual perspective against dualistic interpretations.

The **Ashtavakra Gita**, though not as widely known as the other texts, is a significant scripture in Advaita Vedanta. This dialogue between the sage Ashtavakra and King Janaka explores the nature of self-realization and the illusory nature of the world. The Ashtavakra Gita is celebrated for its clarity and directness, offering profound insights into the nature of consciousness and liberation.

These sacred texts form the bedrock of Advaita Vedanta, guiding seekers toward the realization of their true nature. Through study, contemplation, and practice, these scriptures continue to illuminate the path to non-dual awareness, offering timeless wisdom for spiritual growth and transformation.

**The Eternal Truth of Non-Duality**

In the teachings of Advaita Vedanta, we find ourselves standing at the threshold of a profound realization: the essence of existence is unity, a seamless, non-dual reality that transcends the apparent separateness of our everyday experiences. Advaita Vedanta, with its emphasis on the oneness of Atman (the self) and Brahman (the ultimate reality), invites us to look beyond the illusions of the material world and recognize the eternal truth that underlies all of creation.

In a world where we often feel fragmented and disconnected, the teachings of Advaita Vedanta offer a path back to wholeness. By understanding that our true nature is not separate from the divine but is, in fact, one with it, we can begin to dissolve the barriers of ego and ignorance that keep us bound to the cycle of suffering.

The practical implications of this realization are profound. As we integrate the wisdom of non-duality into our lives, we start to see the world through a different lens—one that is grounded in compassion, humility, and a deep sense of interconnectedness. The divisions that once seemed so insurmountable begin to fade, and we find ourselves moving towards a state of inner peace and spiritual fulfillment.

**Buddhist Mysticism**

## Chapter 2: Buddhist Mysticism

### Section 1. Vajrayana Path

The Vajrayana, often referred to as the "Diamond Vehicle" or "Thunderbolt Vehicle," represents one of the most esoteric and transformative paths within Buddhism. It's a tradition rich with symbolism, ritual, and practices designed to accelerate the journey to enlightenment, offering methods believed to lead to spiritual awakening within a single lifetime.

Imagine a path where every step is looked upon with meaning—where even the most ordinary actions are transformed into opportunities for profound spiritual growth. This is the essence of Vajrayana, a tradition that views the challenges of life not as obstacles to be avoided but as tools for deepening one's understanding of the mind and the nature of reality.

The Vajrayana path emerged from the Mahayana tradition and took root in Tibet, where it flourished and became deeply intertwined with the culture and spiritual life of the region. Unlike other forms of Buddhism that emphasize gradual progress over many lifetimes, Vajrayana offers a more direct approach. It uses powerful methods—sometimes referred to as "skillful means" (*Upaya*)—to help practitioners experience the ultimate truth of non-duality and the inherent Buddha nature within themselves.

Central to Vajrayana is the idea that the mind has both ordinary and enlightened aspects. The practices in this tradition aim to reveal the mind's true nature, which is already pure and luminous, but often obscured by ignorance, attachments, and negative emotions. Vajrayana teaches that by recognizing and working with these obscurations, rather than rejecting them, practitioners can transform them into wisdom and compassion.

One of the unique aspects of Vajrayana is its emphasis on direct experience through rituals and meditative practices. These are not merely symbolic but are considered actual processes of transformation. For instance, in Deity Yoga, practitioners visualize themselves as a particular deity, embodying the qualities of that deity. This practice is based on the belief that all beings possess the potential for Buddhahood and that by identifying with an enlightened deity, one can accelerate the realization of this potential.

Another key element of Vajrayana is the Guru-disciple relationship. The Guru is seen as the embodiment of all the Buddhas, and the connection between the Guru and the disciple is considered essential for the successful transmission of Vajrayana teachings. The Guru provides the disciple with initiations, or empowerments, which are necessary to practice the advanced techniques of Vajrayana. These initiations are not simply formal ceremonies; they are believed to be transformative experiences that plant the seeds of enlightenment in the disciple's mindstream.

The Vajrayana path also includes practices like Mahamudra and Dzogchen, which are considered the pinnacle of Vajrayana teachings. These practices focus on recognizing the nature of the mind directly, without relying on conceptual frameworks or elaborate rituals. Mahamudra, often associated with the Kagyu school, and Dzogchen, central to the Nyingma tradition, both emphasize the realization of the mind's innate clarity and emptiness—its ultimate nature.

Vajrayana Buddhism is also known for its use of mandalas, mantras, and mudras—sacred symbols, sounds, and gestures that are used to invoke the presence of enlightened beings and to transform the practitioner's environment into a pure realm. The creation and contemplation of mandalas, for example, are practices that help the practitioner visualize the universe as a manifestation of the divine, reinforcing the non-dual nature of reality.

At its core, Vajrayana is about transformation—transforming the ordinary into the sacred, ignorance into wisdom, and suffering into enlightenment. It's a path that demands deep commitment and discipline but offers the promise of profound spiritual awakening. For those who walk the Vajrayana path, every moment becomes an opportunity to see through the illusions of the ordinary world and to experience the radiant clarity of the enlightened mind.

### Section 2. Core Practices

The practices in Vajrayana Buddhism are diverse and deeply transformative, designed to engage the practitioner's body, speech, and mind in the journey toward enlightenment. These practices are often complex and require the guidance of a qualified teacher, as they involve powerful techniques that can lead to rapid spiritual progress if practiced correctly.

A. **Deity Yoga:**
Deity Yoga is one of the central practices in Vajrayana. In this practice, the practitioner visualizes themselves as an enlightened deity, such as Tara or Avalokiteshvara, embodying the deity's qualities of wisdom, compassion, and power. This visualization is more than just an imaginative

exercise; it is a profound method for transforming the practitioner's identity from an ordinary, limited self into the divine. By meditating on the deity's form, reciting their mantra, and visualizing their sacred environment, the practitioner dissolves the ordinary perception of reality and experiences the world as a pure manifestation of the divine.

### B. Mandala Meditation:
Mandalas are intricate geometric designs that represent the universe and the mind of the deity. In Vajrayana practice, meditating on a mandala involves visualizing oneself entering the sacred space it represents. This meditation helps the practitioner align their mind with the cosmic order, transforming their perception of the world. The process of creating, contemplating, and eventually dissolving a sand mandala, for example, symbolizes the impermanence of all phenomena and the ultimate emptiness of all forms. It's a practice that teaches non-attachment and the realization that all things are interdependent.

### C. Mantra Recitation:
Mantras are sacred syllables or phrases that carry the vibrational essence of specific deities or enlightened beings. Reciting mantras is a key practice in Vajrayana, believed to purify the mind, speech, and body of the practitioner. Mantras like "Om Mani Padme Hum," associated with Avalokiteshvara, are recited to invoke the deity's presence and to cultivate the qualities they embody. The repetitive chanting of mantras, often accompanied by the use of a mala (prayer beads), helps to focus the mind, align it with the divine, and accumulate spiritual merit.

### D. Guru Yoga:
Guru Yoga is perhaps the most foundational practice in Vajrayana. It involves developing a deep connection with

one's Guru, who is viewed as the embodiment of all enlightened beings. The practice typically involves visualizing the Guru above one's head, merging one's mind with the Guru's enlightened mind, and receiving the Guru's blessings. This practice is seen as essential for receiving the full transmission of Vajrayana teachings, as the Guru's guidance helps to navigate the complexities of the path and to avoid potential pitfalls.

### E. Tummo (Inner Heat) Practice:

Tummo, or the inner heat practice, is part of the Six Yogas of Naropa and is designed to awaken and harness the body's subtle energies. Through specific breathing techniques and visualizations, practitioners generate inner heat that purifies the mind and body, leading to heightened states of awareness. Tummo is also associated with the ability to generate warmth in cold environments, but its true purpose is spiritual transformation, revealing the union of bliss and emptiness—a key insight in Vajrayana Buddhism.

### F. Dzogchen Meditation:

Dzogchen, or the "Great Perfection," is considered the highest and most direct practice in Vajrayana Buddhism, particularly within the Nyingma school. Dzogchen teachings focus on recognizing the natural, primordial state of the mind, which is pure, luminous awareness. The practice involves resting in this natural state without the need for elaborate techniques or rituals. Dzogchen is about direct, non-conceptual insight into the nature of reality, where thoughts and emotions are recognized as manifestations of the mind's inherent clarity and allowed to dissolve naturally. This practice leads to the direct realization of non-duality, where the practitioner experiences the inseparability of samsara (the cycle of existence) and nirvana (liberation).

These core practices form the backbone of Vajrayana Buddhism, offering a powerful means of transforming the practitioner's mind and leading them toward enlightenment. Each practice is designed to engage the practitioner fully, utilizing body, speech, and mind in the pursuit of spiritual awakening. With dedication and the guidance of a skilled teacher, these practices open the door to profound inner transformation and the realization of the ultimate truth.

**Section 3. Philosophical Concepts**

At the heart of Vajrayana Buddhism lies a rich tapestry of philosophical concepts that guide practitioners on their path to enlightenment. These concepts are not just abstract ideas but practical tools that transform the way one perceives reality.

**Emptiness (Śūnyatā):**
One of the most central concepts in Vajrayana is *Śūnyatā*, or emptiness. In Vajrayana, emptiness does not mean nothingness. Instead, it refers to the understanding that all phenomena, including the self, lack inherent, independent existence. Everything is interconnected, arising and existing in relation to everything else. This realization of emptiness is crucial because it frees the practitioner from the attachments and delusions that bind them to the cycle of suffering, allowing them to perceive the true nature of reality.

**Clear Light (Prabhāsvara):**
Another profound concept is that of *Prabhāsvara*, or the clear light. This is the inherent, pure awareness that is the true nature of the mind. In Vajrayana practice, recognizing this clear light within oneself is key to attaining enlightenment. The clear light is always present, even if it is

obscured by the clouds of ignorance and negative emotions. Vajrayana practices aim to reveal this clear light, allowing the practitioner to experience their true, luminous nature.

**Yab-Yum (Union of Wisdom and Compassion):**
*Yab-Yum* is a symbolic representation often seen in Vajrayana iconography, depicting male and female deities in union. This imagery represents the essential union of wisdom and compassion, two qualities that must be developed together on the path to enlightenment. Wisdom, in this context, refers to the understanding of emptiness, while compassion is the active expression of that wisdom in the world. The union of these two aspects is essential for the full realization of enlightenment, as it embodies the inseparability of the ultimate nature of reality and the compassionate actions that arise from that understanding.

**Vajra and Bell:**
In Vajrayana rituals, the *Vajra* and *Bell* are powerful symbols. The Vajra, representing method or skillful means, is indestructible and symbolizes the strength and clarity of the enlightened mind. The Bell represents wisdom, particularly the wisdom of emptiness. The combination of the Vajra and Bell in rituals symbolizes the union of method and wisdom—two qualities that must be developed in tandem on the spiritual path. Without wisdom, methods are ineffective, and without methods, wisdom remains abstract and unmanifested.

**The Three Bodies of Buddha (Trikāya):**
Vajrayana Buddhism also teaches the concept of the *Trikāya*, or the three bodies of the Buddha. These are the *Dharmakāya* (truth body), representing the Buddha's ultimate nature as pure, formless awareness; the

*Sambhogakāya* (enjoyment body), representing the Buddha's blissful, celestial form experienced in deep meditation; and the *Nirmāṇakāya* (emanation body), representing the Buddha's physical presence in the world. This concept emphasizes the Buddha's presence in various forms, accessible to beings at different levels of spiritual realization.

These philosophical concepts are not just intellectual exercises but serve as the foundation for Vajrayana's transformative practices. They guide practitioners in understanding the nature of reality, helping them to transcend ordinary perceptions and experience the world as a manifestation of the divine.

### Section 4. Historical Masters

Vajrayana Buddhism has been shaped by a lineage of extraordinary masters whose teachings and practices continue to inspire and guide practitioners today. These historical figures are revered not only for their wisdom but also for their ability to transmit profound spiritual truths.

### Padmasambhava (Guru Rinpoche):

Padmasambhava, often called Guru Rinpoche, is one of the most venerated figures in Vajrayana Buddhism. He is credited with establishing Buddhism in Tibet during the 8th century and is considered the second Buddha in the Tibetan tradition. Padmasambhava's teachings emphasized the importance of both wisdom and compassion and introduced the esoteric practices of Vajrayana to Tibet. He is also known for his role in subduing the local spirits of Tibet, transforming them into protectors of the Dharma. His teachings, particularly those related to Dzogchen (the Great

Perfection), continue to be central to many Vajrayana lineages.

**Milarepa:**
Milarepa, a 12th-century Tibetan yogi, is celebrated for his incredible life story and spiritual accomplishments. After a troubled youth spent practicing black magic, Milarepa turned to the Dharma under the guidance of his teacher, Marpa. Through years of intense meditation and ascetic practice in the mountains, Milarepa attained full enlightenment. He is renowned for his spiritual songs (dohas), which convey the profound insights he gained during his meditative experiences. Milarepa's life is a powerful testament to the possibility of redemption and the transformative power of spiritual practice.

**Tsongkhapa:**
Tsongkhapa (1357-1419) was a highly influential Tibetan scholar and the founder of the Gelug school of Tibetan Buddhism, which later became the dominant school in Tibet. Tsongkhapa is known for his extensive writings on philosophy, monastic discipline, and the integration of Sutra and Tantra practices. His teachings on the Lamrim, or the Stages of the Path to Enlightenment, are still widely studied and practiced today. Tsongkhapa's synthesis of Madhyamaka philosophy and Vajrayana practice has had a lasting impact on the development of Tibetan Buddhism, making his work essential for any serious Vajrayana practitioner.

**Naropa:**
Naropa was an 11th-century Indian scholar and tantric master who is best known for his Six Yogas, a set of advanced tantric practices that include Tummo (inner heat), Dream Yoga, and Phowa (transference of consciousness).

Naropa's teachings have been passed down through the Kagyu lineage of Tibetan Buddhism, where they are still practiced today as essential techniques for attaining enlightenment. Naropa's life and teachings exemplify the profound transformation that is possible through the Vajrayana path, combining rigorous practice with deep philosophical insight.

These historical masters have left a profound legacy in Vajrayana Buddhism. Their lives and teachings continue to guide practitioners on the path to enlightenment, serving as beacons of wisdom, compassion, and spiritual power.

**Section 5. The Tibetan Book of the Dead**

The *Tibetan Book of the Dead*, known in Tibetan as the *Bardo Thödol*, is one of the most famous and revered texts in Vajrayana Buddhism. It offers profound insights into the nature of death, the process of dying, and the transition between death and rebirth. Traditionally, this text is read aloud to the dying or deceased to guide their consciousness through the intermediate states, or *bardos*, that occur after death.

The *Bardo Thödol* is attributed to Padmasambhava and was hidden as a treasure text (terma) by his disciple, Yeshe Tsogyal, to be discovered at a later time by tertöns (treasure finders). The text is structured as a series of instructions given to the consciousness of the deceased, describing the various experiences they will encounter in the bardo state. These include visions of peaceful and wrathful deities, the dissolution of the physical body, and the opportunity to recognize the clear light of ultimate reality.

A central theme of the *Tibetan Book of the Dead* is the importance of recognizing the clear light at the moment of death. This clear light represents the true nature of mind—pure, luminous awareness. If the deceased can recognize this clear light, they can achieve liberation from the cycle of rebirth and attain Buddhahood. However, if the clear light is not recognized, the consciousness continues through the bardo states, eventually leading to rebirth based on karmic tendencies.

The *Bardo Thödol* also serves as a practical guide for the living, encouraging practitioners to prepare for death through meditation, the cultivation of virtue, and the development of insight into the nature of reality. By familiarizing themselves with the bardo states and the instructions in the text, practitioners can approach death with greater awareness and clarity, increasing their chances of achieving liberation.

Beyond its religious significance, the *Tibetan Book of the Dead* has had a significant impact on Western thought, influencing fields as diverse as psychology, spirituality, and the arts. Its teachings on death, rebirth, and the nature of consciousness offer a unique perspective on the journey of the soul, making it one of the most important texts in the Vajrayana tradition.

The teachings and practices of Vajrayana Buddhism invite us to see the world through a different lens—a lens that reveals the interconnectedness of all things and the possibility of transformation in every moment. Through its profound philosophical concepts, the guidance of enlightened masters, and the sacred rituals that guide us through life and death, Vajrayana offers a path of deep insight and rapid spiritual awakening.

Let us reflect on the core message of Vajrayana: that enlightenment is not a distant goal, but a present reality waiting to be realized. The path may be complex and demanding, but it is also deeply rewarding, offering the promise of liberation and the experience of our true, luminous nature.

In embracing the teachings of Vajrayana, we are reminded that the journey to enlightenment is not about transcending the world but about transforming our experience of it. By recognizing the sacred in the everyday and the divine within ourselves, we begin to walk the path of the Vajrayana, where every step brings us closer to the ultimate truth.

**Kabbalah: Jewish Mysticism**

## Chapter 3: Kabbalah: Jewish Mysticism

## Section 1: Origins and Evolution

Kabbalah, often referred to as the mystical branch of Judaism, traces its roots back to ancient times, intertwining with the broader history of Jewish thought and tradition. Its origins are shrouded in mystery, with various strands of mystical practice emerging throughout Jewish history. The word "Kabbalah" itself means "to receive," indicating the transmission of hidden wisdom from teacher to student, often through oral tradition.

Kabbalah's early roots can be found in the esoteric interpretations of the Torah, where scholars sought to uncover the divine secrets hidden within sacred texts. This mystical inclination was present in the prophetic traditions of ancient Israel, where visions and divine encounters hinted at deeper spiritual realities. However, Kabbalah as we know it began to take a more defined shape in the early medieval period, particularly in 12th-century Provence and Spain.

The evolution of Kabbalah was heavily influenced by the social, political, and religious environments of the Jewish communities in these regions. During this time, Jewish scholars were in contact with Islamic and Christian mystics, which further enriched the development of Kabbalistic thought. One of the most significant milestones in Kabbalah's evolution was the emergence of the Zohar, a mystical commentary on the Torah, written in the late 13th century by the Spanish-Jewish mystic Moses de León. The Zohar became the foundational text of Kabbalistic study, offering profound insights into the nature of God, the universe, and the soul.

Over the centuries, Kabbalah continued to evolve, particularly in the context of the Jewish diaspora. The 16th-century city of Safed in Galilee became a major center of Kabbalistic thought, with figures like Isaac Luria (the Ari) further developing its teachings. Lurianic Kabbalah, as it became known, introduced concepts such as *Tzimtzum* (the contraction of God to create space for the universe), *Shevirat HaKelim* (the breaking of the vessels), and *Tikkun Olam* (the repair of the world), which became central to Kabbalistic theology.

Kabbalah's influence spread beyond the confines of Jewish communities, impacting Christian mysticism and Western esotericism in the Renaissance and beyond. Today, Kabbalah remains a living tradition, studied and practiced by those seeking to connect with the divine and explore the mysteries of existence.

## Section 2: Symbolism and Concepts

At the heart of Kabbalistic thought lies a rich tapestry of symbols and concepts, each serving as a key to unlocking the mysteries of the universe and the divine. The most prominent of these symbols is the Tree of Life (*Etz Chaim*), a diagram representing the structure of the universe and the process of creation. The Tree of Life consists of ten spheres, known as Sephirot, each representing a different attribute or emanation of God.

The Sephirot are arranged in three columns, representing the balance between opposing forces: mercy and judgment, compassion and severity, expansion and contraction. At the top of the Tree is Keter, the crown, symbolizing the pure, unmanifest potential of the divine. From Keter, the divine energy flows down through the Sephirot, eventually reaching Malkhut, the kingdom, which represents the physical world and the manifestation of God in creation.

Each Sephira is associated with specific qualities and has a symbolic correspondence to aspects of the human soul, the physical universe, and divine attributes. For example, Chokhmah (Wisdom) and Binah (Understanding) represent the intellectual faculties, while Chesed (Kindness) and Gevurah (Strength) correspond to emotional and ethical dimensions.

Kabbalistic symbolism extends beyond the Tree of Life. The Hebrew alphabet, for instance, is imbued with deep mystical significance, with each letter representing different spiritual energies. The act of creation itself is seen as God speaking the universe into existence, with the Hebrew letters forming the building blocks of reality.

Another central concept in Kabbalah is the idea of divine light. According to Kabbalistic thought, God's infinite light (*Or Ein Sof*) was initially all-encompassing, but through the process of Tzimtzum, God contracted this light to make space for the world. This light was then refracted through the Sephirot, creating the diverse forms of existence we perceive.

Kabbalah also teaches that humanity has a role in the cosmic process of *Tikkun*, or repair. Through righteous living, prayer, and mystical practice, individuals can restore the broken vessels of divine light and bring the world closer to spiritual wholeness.

These symbols and concepts are not merely abstract ideas; they serve as tools for spiritual growth and self-realization. By meditating on the Sephirot, contemplating the divine light, and understanding the mystical significance of Hebrew letters, practitioners of Kabbalah seek to align themselves with the divine and uncover the hidden truths of existence.

## Section 3: Mystical Texts

Kabbalah, like any profound spiritual tradition, is grounded in a rich body of mystical texts that have been revered and studied for centuries. Among these texts, the Zohar stands as the most central and influential. Written in a mystical Aramaic that intertwines with Hebrew, the Zohar is attributed to Rabbi Shimon bar Yochai, though modern scholarship often places its authorship in the 13th century, penned by the Spanish mystic Moses de León. The Zohar is not merely a commentary on the Torah but an esoteric exploration of the divine mysteries embedded within the sacred text.

The Zohar is organized into multiple volumes and covers a vast array of topics, from the nature of God and the creation of the universe to the intricacies of the human soul and the journey toward spiritual enlightenment. It presents a complex cosmology where the visible and invisible worlds are interconnected, and every detail in the Torah has a hidden, mystical meaning. The Zohar's teachings are often presented as dialogues between Rabbi Shimon and his disciples, exploring deep spiritual concepts in a narrative format that invites readers to journey alongside the characters.

Another significant text in Kabbalistic literature is the *Sefer Yetzirah*, or the "Book of Creation." This enigmatic work, one of the earliest Kabbalistic texts, delves into the creation of the universe through the combination of the ten Sephirot and the 22 letters of the Hebrew alphabet. The *Sefer Yetzirah* introduces the idea that the letters of the alphabet are not merely tools for communication but divine instruments through which God created the cosmos. Each letter holds a unique power, and their combinations form the fabric of reality. This text also lays the foundation for the practice of *Gematria*, the mystical interpretation of words and phrases through numerical values.

The *Sefer HaBahir*, or "Book of Brightness," is another foundational text in Kabbalah. Although it is much shorter than the Zohar, the *Sefer HaBahir* is packed with mystical wisdom. It is often considered one of the earliest texts to introduce the concept of the Sephirot as divine emanations, and it plays a critical role in shaping the symbolic and conceptual framework of later Kabbalistic thought. The text is characterized by its cryptic and fragmented style, which invites deep contemplation and interpretation.

These mystical texts are not simply read; they are studied and meditated upon, with each word and phrase holding layers of meaning. They provide the intellectual and spiritual scaffolding for Kabbalistic practice, offering insights into the nature of God, the universe, and the soul's journey toward enlightenment.

### Section 4: Practical Kabbalah

While much of Kabbalah is focused on theoretical and contemplative aspects, there exists a branch known as Practical Kabbalah, which involves the application of mystical principles to affect change in the physical and spiritual realms. Unlike the meditative and speculative practices, Practical Kabbalah has often been viewed with caution due to its potential for misuse.

Practical Kabbalah includes a variety of techniques, such as the creation of amulets, the recitation of sacred names, and the use of divine invocations. These practices are believed to harness the divine energies of the Sephirot and channel them for specific purposes, whether for protection, healing, or spiritual empowerment. For example, certain Kabbalistic amulets are inscribed with combinations of Hebrew letters or names of angels, each chosen for their unique vibrational qualities and their ability to attract or repel certain energies.

One of the central practices of Practical Kabbalah is the use of divine names. In Kabbalistic tradition, the names of God and the angels are seen as powerful tools for connecting with the divine and influencing the spiritual realm. The *Shem HaMephorash*, or the "Explicit Name," is one of the most potent of these divine names, composed of 72 letters derived from three verses in the Book of Exodus. Each combination of letters is associated with a specific angel or spiritual force and can be invoked through prayer or meditation to achieve various spiritual and material outcomes.

Another aspect of Practical Kabbalah is the use of sacred geometry and the Tree of Life in ritual practices. Kabbalists may visualize or meditate upon the Tree of Life, focusing on specific Sephirot to draw down their divine energies. These practices are often accompanied by the recitation of Psalms, blessings, or specific Kabbalistic formulas that align the practitioner with the divine flow of energy.

However, Kabbalistic authorities have often warned against the dangers of Practical Kabbalah, emphasizing that it should only be practiced by those with a deep understanding of its principles and a pure heart. The misuse of these practices, it is believed, can lead to spiritual imbalance or even harm. For this reason, Practical Kabbalah has traditionally been reserved for the most advanced and righteous practitioners, those who have undergone years of spiritual and ethical refinement.

## Section 5: Meditation and Gematria

Meditation in Kabbalah is a profound practice aimed at elevating the soul and connecting with the divine. Unlike the meditative practices of other traditions, Kabbalistic meditation often involves intense concentration on sacred texts, divine names, and the symbolic structures of the Sephirot. Through meditation, the Kabbalist seeks to transcend the physical world and ascend through the levels of spiritual reality, ultimately reaching a state of unity with God.

One of the key techniques in Kabbalistic meditation is *Hitbodedut*, or self-seclusion, which involves withdrawing from the distractions of the world to focus entirely on God. This practice can be done in solitude, often in nature, where the practitioner engages in deep prayer, contemplation, and the recitation of Psalms. The goal of *Hitbodedut* is to achieve a state of *Devekut*, or cleaving to God, where the soul experiences an intimate connection with the divine presence.

Another powerful meditative tool in Kabbalah is *Gematria*, the mystical interpretation of Hebrew words and phrases through their numerical values. In Hebrew, each letter has a corresponding numerical value, and by analyzing these values, Kabbalists uncover hidden connections and meanings within the sacred texts. For example, the word "chai" (life) has a numerical value of 18, which is why the number 18 is considered auspicious in Jewish tradition. Through *Gematria*, the Kabbalist meditates on the numerical relationships between words, unlocking deeper layers of meaning and gaining insight into the divine will.

*Gematria* is not just an intellectual exercise; it is a meditative practice that deepens the Kabbalist's understanding of the interconnectedness of all things. By contemplating the numerical values and their associations, the practitioner enters a state of expanded consciousness, where the boundaries between the physical and spiritual worlds begin to dissolve. This meditative practice allows the Kabbalist to perceive the divine blueprint of creation and align themselves more closely with its purpose.

Kabbalah is a vast and intricate tradition that offers a profound exploration of the mysteries of existence. Through its mystical texts, symbolic frameworks, and practical applications, Kabbalah provides a path to spiritual enlightenment that is both deeply intellectual and intensely experiential. Whether through the study of the Zohar, the practice of meditative techniques, or the application of divine names, Kabbalah invites practitioners to embark on a journey of inner transformation and divine connection.

We have explored the origins and evolution of Kabbalah, delved into its rich symbolism, and examined the ways in which Kabbalists have sought to engage with the divine through practical and meditative practices. These aspects of Kabbalah are not isolated; they form a cohesive spiritual system that integrates the mind, body, and soul, offering a comprehensive approach to understanding and experiencing the divine.

As we move forward, let us carry with us the insights gained from Kabbalah—its emphasis on the interconnectedness of all things, the importance of balancing the spiritual and the material, and the potential for every individual to participate in the divine act of creation and restoration. Kabbalah teaches us that the path to God is not linear but multifaceted, requiring both deep contemplation and active engagement with the world. In embracing this path, we open ourselves to the infinite possibilities of spiritual growth and transformation.

**Christian Mysticism**

## Chapter 4: Christian Mysticism

## Section 1: Early Mystics

Christian mysticism, with its deep roots in the early centuries of the Church, represents a rich tapestry of spiritual exploration and divine union. From the outset, Christian mystics have sought a direct, experiential relationship with God, often transcending the formal doctrines and practices of the institutional Church. Their lives and writings offer a glimpse into the profound inner journeys that have shaped Christian spirituality across the ages.

One of the earliest figures in Christian mysticism is St. Anthony the Great, known as the "Father of All Monks." Born in Egypt in the 3rd century, St. Anthony retreated to the desert to live a life of asceticism and prayer, seeking solitude to commune more deeply with God. His life, as recorded by St. Athanasius in the *Life of Anthony*, became a model for Christian monasticism and inspired countless others to seek God in the silence of the desert. St. Anthony's mysticism was rooted in his intense prayer life, his battles with spiritual temptation, and his unwavering commitment to live in the presence of God.

Another towering figure in early Christian mysticism is St. Augustine of Hippo. While not a mystic in the conventional sense, Augustine's spiritual journey, chronicled in his *Confessions*, laid the groundwork for much of Christian mystical thought. Augustine's profound encounter with God, his reflections on the nature of sin and grace, and his exploration of the inner life have deeply influenced the mystical tradition. His famous phrase, "Our hearts are restless until they rest in You," captures the essence of the mystical quest for divine union.

In the Eastern Christian tradition, St. Gregory of Nyssa stands out as a key mystical thinker. A 4th-century bishop and theologian, Gregory's mystical theology is deeply rooted in the concept of *theosis*, or divinization, where the goal of the Christian life is to become one with God. Gregory's writings, particularly his *Life of Moses*, offer a profound allegory of the soul's journey toward God, emphasizing the endless ascent toward divine perfection. For Gregory, the mystical path is marked by a deepening knowledge of God that paradoxically leads to the realization of God's incomprehensibility, a theme that resonates throughout Eastern Christian mysticism.

Moving into the medieval period, we encounter figures like St. Hildegard of Bingen, a Benedictine abbess and visionary who profoundly impacted Christian mysticism and spirituality. Hildegard's mystical experiences, which she described as visions of divine light, were captured in her works, including *Scivias* and *Liber Divinorum Operum*. Her visions, filled with rich symbolism and theological insights, reflected a deep connection with the divine and offered profound reflections on the nature of creation, humanity, and the cosmos. Hildegard's mysticism was not just contemplative but also deeply prophetic, as she believed her visions were messages from God meant to guide and reform the Church.

Another significant medieval mystic is Meister Eckhart, a German Dominican friar and theologian whose sermons and writings have left an indelible mark on Christian mysticism. Eckhart's mysticism centered on the idea of the "ground" of the soul, where God and the soul are united in a profound, direct experience of the divine. His teachings on detachment, the birth of God in the soul, and the soul's return to its divine source challenged conventional religious thought and emphasized the possibility of experiencing God within oneself. Despite facing accusations of heresy, Eckhart's mystical theology has continued to inspire and influence Christian mystics to this day.

St. John of the Cross and St. Teresa of Ávila, both key figures in the Spanish mysticism of the 16th century, represent the pinnacle of Christian mystical writing. John's poetry and writings, particularly the *Dark Night of the Soul*, explore the painful yet transformative process of spiritual purification and union with God. Teresa's works, including *The Interior Castle*, offer a detailed roadmap of the soul's journey through various stages of prayer and mystical union. Together, they formed the backbone of the Carmelite Reform, emphasizing a return to contemplative prayer and the pursuit of direct experience of God.

These early Christian mystics, through their writings and spiritual practices, laid the foundation for a rich tradition of mystical theology that continues to inspire believers today. Their lives demonstrate that the mystical path is one of both profound joy and deep suffering, as the soul seeks to transcend the material world and enter into the ineffable presence of God.

**Section 2: Key Practices**

Christian mysticism is not just a theoretical or theological pursuit; it is deeply rooted in practices that cultivate a direct, experiential relationship with God. These practices, developed and refined over centuries, serve as pathways to divine union, helping mystics transcend the ordinary and enter into the mystical.

One of the most central practices in Christian mysticism is contemplative prayer, also known as "silent" or "centering" prayer. Unlike vocal or petitionary prayer, contemplative prayer involves resting in the presence of God, beyond words and thoughts. The goal of this practice is to enter into a state of stillness where the soul can encounter God directly. This form of prayer has its roots in the early Christian monastic tradition, particularly among the Desert Fathers and Mothers, who sought God in silence and solitude. Contemplative prayer was further developed by mystics like St. Teresa of Ávila and St. John of the Cross, who described it as an intimate communion with God that goes beyond the senses and intellect.

Another key practice is the use of meditation on Scripture, also known as *Lectio Divina*, or "divine reading." This ancient practice involves slowly and prayerfully reading passages from the Bible, allowing the words to sink deeply into the heart and mind. The process typically involves four steps: *lectio* (reading), *meditatio* (meditation), *oratio* (prayer), and *contemplatio* (contemplation). Through this practice, the mystic seeks to encounter God in the sacred text, allowing the Holy Spirit to speak through the words and guide the soul into deeper understanding and union with God.

The sacraments, particularly the Eucharist, play a vital role in Christian mystical practice. The Eucharist, understood as the real presence of Christ in the bread and wine, is seen by mystics as a profound encounter with the divine. Participation in the Eucharist is not merely a ritual act but a mystical experience where the believer is united with Christ in a tangible and intimate way. For mystics like St. Catherine of Siena and Julian of Norwich, the Eucharist was a central focus of their spiritual lives, offering them a direct experience of God's love and grace.

Mystical theology also emphasizes the practice of *via negativa*, or the "negative way," which involves approaching God by stripping away all images, concepts, and attachments that can obscure the divine presence. This apophatic approach, advocated by mystics like Meister Eckhart and the author of *The Cloud of Unknowing*, teaches that God is ultimately beyond all human understanding and that the path to union with God involves letting go of all preconceived notions and entering into the "unknowing" or "darkness" of God's mystery. Through this process of negation, the soul can move closer to God, who is beyond all that can be spoken or imagined.

Mystical asceticism is another important practice in Christian mysticism, particularly in the monastic tradition. Ascetic practices such as fasting, vigils, and bodily disciplines are seen as ways to purify the soul and detach from the desires of the flesh, allowing the mystic to focus entirely on the pursuit of God. While asceticism is often associated with physical discipline, its deeper purpose is spiritual—by denying oneself, the mystic seeks to empty the soul of all that is not God, creating space for divine grace to enter.

Finally, mystics often engage in the practice of *visions* and *revelations*, which are seen as direct communications from God. Throughout Christian history, many mystics have reported receiving visions of Christ, the Virgin Mary, or other divine figures, often during deep prayer or contemplation. These visions are not just private experiences but are often shared with the wider community as sources of inspiration, guidance, and prophecy. St. Hildegard of Bingen, for example, recorded her visions in elaborate detail, and they became a source of spiritual wisdom for her time and beyond.

These key practices of Christian mysticism are not isolated activities but are deeply interconnected, each contributing to the mystic's journey toward divine union. Through prayer, meditation, asceticism, and visionary experiences, Christian mystics have sought to draw closer to God, experiencing the divine presence in profound and transformative ways.

## Section 3: Prominent Figures

Christian mysticism has been shaped by a rich tapestry of influential figures whose lives and writings have left an indelible mark on the spiritual landscape. These mystics, each with their unique experiences and teachings, have contributed to the depth and diversity of Christian mystical thought.

One of the most influential figures in Christian mysticism is St. Teresa of Ávila. A 16th-century Spanish mystic and reformer of the Carmelite order, Teresa is best known for her profound spiritual writings and her role in the Catholic Reformation. Her book *The Interior Castle* offers a detailed map of the soul's journey toward divine union, describing the various "mansions" or stages of spiritual development. Teresa's mysticism is characterized by her emphasis on contemplative prayer, her vivid visions, and her profound sense of intimacy with God. Her teachings on the "prayer of quiet" and the "prayer of union" have become foundational to Christian contemplative practice, influencing countless spiritual seekers.

Another key figure is St. John of the Cross, a close contemporary of St. Teresa and a fellow reformer of the Carmelite order. John's mystical theology is perhaps best captured in his work *The Dark Night of the Soul*, where he describes the soul's journey through the trials of spiritual purification toward the ultimate goal of union with God. John's mysticism is marked by its emphasis on the necessity of suffering and detachment as means to attain spiritual maturity. His poetry and prose explore the paradoxes of divine love, where the soul must undergo profound darkness to reach the light of God's presence. St. John's writings continue to inspire those who seek a deeper understanding of the mystical path, particularly in the context of spiritual trials and growth.

Julian of Norwich, a 14th-century English anchoress, is another towering figure in Christian mysticism. Her book, *Revelations of Divine Love*, is considered one of the most important texts in English spiritual literature. Julian's mystical experiences, centered on her visions of Christ's suffering and the overwhelming love of God, convey a message of hope and divine compassion. Her famous phrase, "All shall be well, and all shall be well, and all manner of thing shall be well," reflects her deep conviction in God's infinite love and mercy. Julian's mysticism is characterized by her emphasis on the maternal aspects of God, her profound trust in divine providence, and her innovative theological insights that continue to resonate with readers today.

In the Eastern Christian tradition, St. Symeon the New Theologian stands out as a significant mystical figure. Living in the 10th and 11th centuries, Symeon's mysticism is marked by his emphasis on the direct, personal experience of the Holy Spirit. His teachings on the "uncreated light" and the transformative power of divine grace were considered radical in his time, yet they deeply influenced Eastern Orthodox spirituality. Symeon's writings, particularly his *Hymns of Divine Love*, express a passionate longing for God and a vivid description of mystical union with the divine. His work laid the groundwork for later Eastern Orthodox mystical traditions, particularly the Hesychast movement, which emphasized inner stillness and the prayer of the heart.

Meister Eckhart, a 13th-century German Dominican friar, represents another key figure in Christian mysticism. Eckhart's sermons and writings explore the concept of the "ground" of the soul, where the soul and God are united in a state beyond all dualities. His teachings on detachment, the "birth of God" within the soul, and the mystical path as one of direct experience of the divine challenged the theological norms of his time. Despite facing accusations of heresy, Eckhart's mystical theology has continued to influence Christian spirituality, particularly in its emphasis on the inner journey toward God.

These prominent figures in Christian mysticism, each with their unique contributions, have helped shape the contours of Christian spiritual thought. Their lives and teachings offer timeless insights into the nature of the divine, the soul's journey, and the profound mysteries of faith.

### Section 4: Mystical Texts

Christian mysticism is deeply rooted in a rich tradition of mystical texts that have guided and inspired countless generations of spiritual seekers. These texts, often written by the mystics themselves, offer profound insights into the nature of God, the soul, and the spiritual journey toward divine union.

One of the most significant mystical texts in Christian history is *The Cloud of Unknowing*, an anonymous 14th-century work that has become a cornerstone of Christian contemplative practice. The text, written as a guide for those seeking to draw closer to God through contemplative prayer, emphasizes the need to let go of all thoughts and images of God, entering instead into the "cloud of unknowing" where God's presence can be experienced directly. The author's teachings on the "cloud of forgetting," where one must forget all created things to focus entirely on God, resonate deeply with those on the mystical path. *The Cloud of Unknowing* has influenced many later mystics, particularly in its emphasis on the apophatic way—the path of unknowing—as a means of encountering the divine.

Another key mystical text is *The Interior Castle* by St. Teresa of Ávila. In this spiritual classic, Teresa describes the soul as a castle made of crystal or diamond, with many rooms or "mansions," each representing different stages of spiritual growth. The journey through the mansions, guided by prayer and the grace of God, leads ultimately to the innermost chamber, where the soul encounters God in intimate union. Teresa's vivid imagery, coupled with her practical advice on the life of prayer, makes *The Interior Castle* a foundational text for those seeking to understand the stages of spiritual development.

St. John of the Cross's *Dark Night of the Soul* is another seminal work in Christian mysticism. In this text, John explores the painful yet transformative process of spiritual purification that the soul must undergo to achieve union with God. The "dark night" refers to the experience of spiritual desolation and emptiness that precedes the soul's entry into the divine presence. John's writings offer profound insights into the nature of suffering, detachment, and the mysterious ways in which God draws the soul closer through trials. The *Dark Night of the Soul* has become a key reference for those experiencing spiritual struggles, offering hope and guidance in the midst of darkness.

In the Eastern Orthodox tradition, the *Philokalia* is a collection of mystical and ascetic writings by various Church Fathers, compiled in the 18th century. The *Philokalia* emphasizes the practice of Hesychasm, a form of contemplative prayer that seeks inner stillness and the continuous remembrance of God. The texts within the *Philokalia* offer practical advice on the spiritual life, particularly the importance of vigilance, humility, and the prayer of the heart. The *Philokalia* has been highly influential in Eastern Christian mysticism, particularly among monastic communities, and continues to be a source of inspiration for those seeking to cultivate a deep, prayerful relationship with God.

These mystical texts, each unique in its approach and emphasis, provide invaluable guidance for those on the Christian mystical path. They offer both practical advice and profound theological insights, helping seekers navigate the complexities of the spiritual journey and draw closer to the divine.

### Section 5: Themes of Union with God

At the heart of Christian mysticism lies the profound and transformative theme of union with God. This concept, often referred to as "divine union" or *theosis* in the Eastern

Christian tradition, is the ultimate goal of the mystical path —a state where the soul is fully united with God, transcending all separation and duality.

The theme of union with God is central to the writings of many Christian mystics. St. Teresa of Ávila describes this union as a "spiritual marriage" in her work *The Interior Castle*, where the soul and God are joined in a profound and intimate relationship. Teresa's imagery of the soul as a bride, and God as the divine bridegroom, captures the deep love and devotion that characterize this union. For Teresa, this state of union is the culmination of the spiritual journey, where the soul experiences the fullness of God's presence and love.

St. John of the Cross also explores the theme of union with God, particularly in his poetry and writings on the *Dark Night of the Soul*. For John, the path to union with God involves a process of purification, where the soul must be stripped of all attachments and desires that separate it from God. This "dark night" is a necessary stage in the journey, leading ultimately to the "transforming union," where the soul becomes one with God in a state of perfect love and peace. John's emphasis on the transformative power of suffering and detachment highlights the challenges and rewards of the mystical path.

In Eastern Christian mysticism, the theme of union with God is often expressed through the concept of *theosis*, or divinization. This idea, rooted in the teachings of the Church Fathers, suggests that the ultimate goal of the Christian life is to become "partakers of the divine nature" (2 Peter 1:4). Through the process of *theosis*, the soul is gradually transformed into the likeness of God, sharing in the divine life and experiencing a profound communion with the Holy

Trinity. This theme is central to the writings of mystics like St. Symeon the New Theologian, who emphasized the direct, personal experience of God's presence and the transformative power of divine grace.

The theme of union with God also appears in the writings of Meister Eckhart, who speaks of the "birth of God in the soul." For Eckhart, this mystical union involves the realization that the true "ground" of the soul is one with the divine ground, where all distinctions between God and the soul disappear. Eckhart's teachings on the "breakthrough" to God emphasize the importance of letting go of the self and all created things to enter into this state of union, where the soul rests in the divine presence.

In Christian mysticism, the theme of union with God is not merely a theological concept but a lived reality—a state of being that transforms the soul and brings it into the fullness of divine love and light. This union is the ultimate goal of the mystical path, offering a vision of the soul's destiny as it is drawn ever closer to the heart of God.

Christian mysticism offers a profound and intricate journey into the depths of spiritual experience, where the ultimate aim is nothing less than union with the Divine. As we've seen, this mystical path has been richly shaped by the lives and teachings of its most prominent figures, the wisdom contained within its foundational texts, and the transformative practices that guide the soul toward its ultimate destiny.

The early Christian mystics, from St. Teresa of Ávila to Meister Eckhart, have shown us that the path to God is both challenging and deeply rewarding. Their writings and experiences provide a roadmap for those who seek to go beyond mere belief to a living, breathing relationship with the Divine. The mystical texts that have emerged from these traditions serve not only as guides but as companions, offering solace and insight along the way.

The practices of Christian mysticism—whether through contemplative prayer, meditation on Scripture, or the ascetic disciplines—are not merely rituals but profound expressions of the soul's yearning for God. These practices help to purify the heart, focus the mind, and open the spirit to the transformative power of divine love. They are the means by which the soul ascends, step by step, closer to the ineffable presence of God.

The theme of union with God stands at the heart of Christian mystical tradition. It is a union that is both deeply personal and universally accessible, offering a glimpse of the divine reality that lies beyond the ordinary world. This union is not just the goal of the mystic but the destiny of every soul, a journey toward the fulfillment of our deepest longings and the realization of our true nature in the divine.

Christian mysticism is not a path for the faint-hearted, but for those who are willing to surrender everything in their pursuit of God. It is a path of deep introspection, profound transformation, and ultimate union—a journey that continues to inspire and guide countless seekers today.

## Sufism: The Islamic Mystical Path

# Chapter 5: Sufism: The Islamic Mystical Path

## Section 1: Sufi Origins

Sufism, often described as the heart of Islam, represents the mystical dimension of the Islamic faith. It is a path that seeks to transcend the outward rituals and doctrines of religion, focusing instead on the inner, spiritual journey toward God. The origins of Sufism are deeply rooted in the early centuries of Islam, emerging as a response to the growing emphasis on legalism and formalism within the religion.

The word "Sufi" is believed to be derived from the Arabic word *suf*, meaning wool, referring to the simple woolen garments worn by early mystics as a symbol of their renunciation of worldly attachments. These early Sufis sought to return to the purity and simplicity of the Prophet Muhammad's teachings, emphasizing personal piety, humility, and the cultivation of a deep, loving relationship with God.

The origins of Sufism can be traced back to the life of the Prophet Muhammad himself, who is considered by Sufis to be the perfect exemplar of mystical spirituality. The Prophet's night journey (*Isra and Mi'raj*), where he ascended through the heavens and came into the presence of God, is seen as a profound mystical experience that serves as the foundation for Sufi spirituality. The Prophet's life, characterized by moments of deep contemplation, prayer, and divine inspiration, set the stage for the development of Islamic mysticism.

In the centuries following the Prophet's death, the early Muslim community faced a period of rapid expansion and the challenges of governance, leading to an increasing emphasis on Islamic law (*Sharia*) and theological debate. Amid this environment, a group of devout Muslims began to emphasize the importance of the inner, spiritual life, seeking to cultivate a direct and personal relationship with God. These early mystics, often referred to as *zuhhad* (ascetics) or *ubbad* (devotees), laid the groundwork for what would later be recognized as Sufism.

One of the earliest and most influential figures in the development of Sufism was Hasan al-Basri (642–728 CE), a renowned scholar and ascetic from Basra, Iraq. Hasan al-Basri's teachings emphasized the importance of living a life of piety, humility, and constant remembrance of God (*dhikr*). He spoke of the need to detach from worldly desires and focus on the inner purification of the soul, a theme that would become central to Sufi thought. Hasan al-Basri's emphasis on *tawakkul* (trust in God) and *zuhd* (asceticism) deeply influenced subsequent generations of Sufis.

Another pivotal figure in the early development of Sufism was Rabia al-Adawiyya (713–801 CE), a female mystic from Basra who is revered for her intense devotion and love for God. Rabia's teachings focused on the concept of divine love (*mahabbah*), emphasizing that the ultimate goal of the spiritual path is to love God for God's sake alone, without any desire for reward or fear of punishment. Her poetry and sayings, filled with expressions of longing and intimacy with the divine, have become iconic in Sufi literature. Rabia's emphasis on selfless love and her rejection of materialism further shaped the ethos of Sufism.

As Sufism continued to develop, it began to take on more formalized structures, with the establishment of *tariqas* (Sufi orders) that provided spiritual guidance and community for seekers. These orders were often founded by charismatic Sufi masters who attracted disciples and established centers of learning and worship. One of the most famous of these early Sufi masters was Abu Hamid al-Ghazali (1058–1111 CE), a renowned theologian, philosopher, and mystic. Al-Ghazali's work, particularly his magnum opus *Ihya Ulum al-Din* (The Revival of the Religious Sciences), integrated Sufism with mainstream Islamic thought, bridging the gap between mysticism and orthodoxy. Al-Ghazali's teachings on the purification of the heart, the importance of sincerity in worship, and the need for inner transformation had a profound impact on the development of Sufism.

By the 12th century, Sufism had spread across the Islamic world, from North Africa to Central Asia, deeply influencing the spiritual and cultural life of Muslim communities. Sufi poets, such as Jalal al-Din Rumi and Fariduddin Attar, expressed the mystical experiences and insights of Sufism in beautiful and evocative verse, further popularizing the mystical path. Sufi saints, known as *wali* or *friends of God*, were revered for their spiritual wisdom and miraculous powers, and their tombs became pilgrimage sites for devotees seeking blessings and spiritual guidance.

Sufism's origins, deeply rooted in the life of the Prophet Muhammad and the early Islamic community, represent a continuous thread of mystical spirituality that has evolved and adapted over the centuries. It remains a vibrant and dynamic force within Islam, offering a path of love, devotion, and inner transformation for those who seek to draw closer to God.

## Section 2: Spiritual Practices

At the heart of Sufism lies a rich array of spiritual practices designed to bring the seeker closer to God and cultivate a deep, experiential knowledge of the divine. These practices, which have been developed and refined over centuries, form the core of the Sufi path, guiding the soul toward purification, enlightenment, and union with the Beloved.

One of the most central practices in Sufism is *dhikr*, or the remembrance of God. *Dhikr* involves the repetition of divine names, phrases from the Quran, or other sacred invocations, with the goal of keeping the presence of God constantly in the heart and mind. This practice can be performed individually or in a group, often accompanied by rhythmic movements, breathing exercises, and music to help deepen the state of spiritual awareness. The repetition of *dhikr* is believed to cleanse the heart of worldly distractions and open it to the light of divine presence. Sufis often describe *dhikr* as a way of polishing the heart's mirror, allowing it to reflect the divine light more clearly.

Another key practice in Sufism is *muraqabah*, or spiritual meditation. *Muraqabah* involves focusing the mind and heart on God, entering into a state of deep contemplation where the self is gradually effaced in the presence of the divine. This practice is often compared to the Christian practice of contemplative prayer, where the goal is not to ask for anything but simply to be present with God. *Muraqabah* can lead to profound spiritual insights and experiences, where the boundaries between the self and the divine begin to dissolve, and the seeker experiences a taste of the unity (*tawhid*) of all things in God.

*Sama*, or spiritual listening, is another important practice in Sufism, particularly among certain Sufi orders like the Mevlevi. *Sama* involves listening to sacred music and poetry, often accompanied by dance, as a way of opening the heart to divine love and ecstasy. The most famous form of *Sama* is the whirling dance of the Mevlevi dervishes, also known as the Whirling Dervishes, who spin in circles as a form of moving meditation, symbolizing the rotation of the planets around the sun and the soul's journey toward God. Through *Sama*, Sufis seek to transcend the ordinary world and enter into a state of spiritual intoxication (*wajd*), where they are overcome by the presence of God.

Fasting (*sawm*) and retreat (*khalwa*) are also important practices in Sufism, used to purify the soul and draw closer to God. Fasting, particularly during the month of Ramadan, is seen as a way of disciplining the body and focusing the mind on God. In addition to the obligatory fasts, Sufis often engage in additional fasting as a form of spiritual discipline. *Khalwa*, or spiritual retreat, involves withdrawing from the distractions of the world to spend time in solitude and prayer. This practice, which can last from a few days to several months, is seen as a way of deepening one's connection with God and receiving spiritual insights. During *khalwa*, the seeker often engages in intense prayer, *dhikr*, and meditation, seeking to empty the self of all that is not God.

The practice of *Ihsan*, or spiritual excellence, is a central concept in Sufism, where the goal is to worship God as if one sees Him, knowing that even if one does not see God, God sees the worshiper. This practice involves striving for perfection in one's worship, character, and actions, with the aim of embodying the divine qualities in daily life. Sufis believe that by practicing *Ihsan*, they can draw closer to God and reflect His attributes in the world.

Sufi practices are not merely ritualistic but are deeply transformative, aimed at purifying the heart, disciplining the soul, and opening the self to the presence of God. These practices, which are at the core of the Sufi path, guide the seeker on a journey of inner transformation, leading ultimately to the realization of the unity and love that underlie all creation.

**Section 3: Sufi Orders**

As Sufism evolved and spread throughout the Islamic world, it began to organize itself into distinct *tariqas*, or Sufi orders, each with its own unique practices, teachings, and spiritual lineage. These orders played a crucial role in the transmission of Sufi wisdom and provided a structured environment for spiritual growth and community.

One of the most prominent Sufi orders is the Qadiriyya, founded by Abd al-Qadir al-Jilani in the 12th century. Al-Jilani, a revered scholar and mystic, emphasized the importance of humility, service to others, and constant remembrance of God. The Qadiriyya order, known for its emphasis on *dhikr* and spiritual discipline, became one of the most widespread Sufi orders, with branches throughout the Islamic world. The Qadiriyya's teachings on love, compassion, and social responsibility continue to resonate with Sufis today, making it one of the most enduring and influential Sufi orders.

Another significant Sufi order is the Naqshbandiyya, which traces its origins to the 14th-century mystic Baha-ud-Din Naqshband in Central Asia. The Naqshbandi order is known for its silent *dhikr* and its emphasis on the "sober" path of Sufism, focusing on inner purity and spiritual awareness without outward displays of ecstasy or ritual. The

Naqshbandi order also places great importance on the concept of *suhba* (companionship), where spiritual guidance is passed directly from master to disciple through close personal relationships. The Naqshbandi order has been particularly influential in the Ottoman Empire and later in modern Turkey, Central Asia, and South Asia, where it continues to be a major force in Sufi spirituality.

The Chishti order, founded by Moinuddin Chishti in the 12th century in India, is another key Sufi order known for its emphasis on love, tolerance, and openness to people of all faiths. The Chishti order is renowned for its beautiful devotional music (*qawwali*), which is used as a form of *Sama* to evoke spiritual ecstasy and divine love. The order's inclusive approach and its focus on serving humanity, especially the poor and marginalized, have made it one of the most popular Sufi orders in South Asia. The Chishti order's influence can be seen in the vibrant Sufi culture that thrives in India and Pakistan today.

The Mevlevi order, founded by the followers of Jalal al-Din Rumi in the 13th century, is perhaps the most famous Sufi order in the West. Known as the Whirling Dervishes, the Mevlevi are renowned for their practice of *Sama*, a form of spiritual dance and music that symbolizes the soul's journey toward God. Rumi's poetry, which expresses the ecstatic love for God and the longing for union with the divine, forms the core of the Mevlevi tradition. The Mevlevi order has played a significant role in spreading Sufism in the West, where Rumi's works have become widely popular and have introduced many to the mystical path of Sufism.

The Bektashi order, which emerged in the 13th century in Anatolia, is another important Sufi order, particularly in the context of Turkish and Balkan Islam. The Bektashi order is known for its syncretic practices, incorporating elements of Shia Islam, Christianity, and local folk traditions. The Bektashi order played a significant role in the spiritual life of the Ottoman Empire, particularly among the Janissaries, the elite military corps of the empire. Today, the Bektashi order continues to be a significant spiritual force in Turkey, Albania, and the Balkans, known for its emphasis on tolerance, inclusivity, and social justice.

These Sufi orders, each with its unique practices and teachings, have contributed to the rich diversity of Sufism and have played a crucial role in preserving and transmitting Sufi wisdom across generations. The orders provide a structured path for spiritual seekers, offering guidance, community, and a deep connection to the mystical tradition of Islam.

### Section 4: Notable Sufis

Throughout the history of Sufism, numerous individuals have stood out for their profound spiritual insights, contributions to Sufi literature, and their roles as teachers and guides. These notable Sufis have not only shaped the development of Sufism but have also left a lasting impact on Islamic spirituality and beyond.

Jalal al-Din Rumi, perhaps the most famous Sufi poet and mystic, is revered not only within the Sufi tradition but also across the world for his deeply spiritual poetry that transcends religious boundaries. Born in 1207 in present-day Afghanistan, Rumi's encounter with the wandering dervish Shams of Tabriz transformed his life and led to the outpouring of poetry that expresses the soul's longing for God. His most famous work, the *Mathnawi*, is often called the "Quran in Persian" for its deep spiritual wisdom. Rumi's teachings on love, unity, and the divine have resonated with people of all backgrounds, making him one of the most beloved poets in history.

Rabia al-Adawiyya, one of the earliest and most influential female Sufis, is known for her teachings on divine love. Born in Basra in the 8th century, Rabia's devotion to God was characterized by her intense love and desire to worship God for His own sake, not out of fear of hell or desire for paradise. Her life of asceticism and her poetry, which speaks of the soul's intimate relationship with God, have inspired generations of Sufis. Rabia's emphasis on selfless love for God continues to be a central theme in Sufi thought and practice.

Al-Hallaj, a 10th-century Sufi mystic and martyr, is remembered for his bold declaration, "Ana al-Haqq" ("I am the Truth"), which was interpreted as a claim to divine union. This statement led to his execution by the Abbasid authorities, but it also cemented his place in Sufi history as a symbol of the ultimate mystical experience of unity with God. Al-Hallaj's life and teachings, particularly his poetry and his emphasis on the annihilation of the self in the divine (*fana*), have deeply influenced later Sufi thought. He is seen as a martyr of divine love, willing to sacrifice everything for his union with God.

Ibn Arabi, known as "The Greatest Master" (*al-Shaykh al-Akbar*), is one of the most important figures in Islamic mysticism. Born in Andalusia in 1165, Ibn Arabi's extensive writings, particularly his magnum opus *Fusus al-Hikam* (The Bezels of Wisdom), explore the nature of reality, the oneness of existence (*wahdat al-wujud*), and the relationship between God and creation. Ibn Arabi's mystical philosophy, which emphasizes the unity of all being and the presence of God in all things, has had a profound influence on Sufism and Islamic thought as a whole. His teachings continue to inspire and challenge Sufi seekers to this day.

Abd al-Qadir al-Jilani, the founder of the Qadiriyya order, is another prominent figure in Sufi history. Born in 1077 in Persia, al-Jilani's teachings emphasized the importance of humility, charity, and constant remembrance of God. He became known for his miraculous powers and his ability to draw large numbers of followers to the Sufi path. Al-Jilani's influence extends beyond the Qadiriyya order, as his teachings and example have inspired countless Sufis across the Islamic world.

These notable Sufis, each with their unique contributions, have shaped the spiritual landscape of Sufism and left a lasting legacy that continues to inspire and guide seekers on the mystical path.

### Section 5: Concepts of Fana and Baqa

Central to Sufi metaphysics are the twin concepts of *fana* (annihilation) and *baqa* (subsistence), which describe the stages of the soul's journey toward union with God. These concepts are foundational to understanding the mystical process in Sufism, representing the transformative experiences that lead the seeker to a deeper relationship with the Divine.

*Fana* refers to the annihilation of the ego or the self in the presence of God. It is the process by which the Sufi experiences the dissolution of individual identity, realizing the nothingness of the self in comparison to the infinite reality of God. This state is often described as a mystical death, where the seeker is consumed by the divine presence, losing all sense of personal will, desires, and consciousness of the material world. The experience of *fana* is a profound moment of spiritual realization, where the soul recognizes that there is no existence except God, and all creation is merely a reflection of the Divine.

However, *fana* is not the final stage of the mystical journey. Following the experience of *fana* comes *baqa*, which refers to the state of subsistence or permanence in God. After the ego has been annihilated, the Sufi is reborn in the presence of God, not as an independent self, but as one who subsists through God. In *baqa*, the seeker returns to the world with a transformed consciousness, where the individual's actions, thoughts, and existence are entirely aligned with the Divine will. It is a state of spiritual maturity and completeness, where the Sufi lives in a constant awareness of God's presence and acts as a vessel of divine love and mercy in the world.

The interplay between *fana* and *baqa* is central to Sufi thought, reflecting the dynamic relationship between the self and the Divine. While *fana* emphasizes the need to transcend the ego and worldly attachments, *baqa* highlights the return to the world with a renewed sense of purpose and divine consciousness. Together, these concepts illustrate the cyclical nature of the mystical path, where the Sufi continually experiences moments of annihilation and subsistence as they draw closer to God.

The concepts of *fana* and *baqa* have been explored and elaborated upon by numerous Sufi masters, including Al-Hallaj, Ibn Arabi, and Rumi, each contributing to the rich tapestry of Sufi metaphysical thought. These concepts continue to be central to Sufi practice and philosophy, offering profound insights into the nature of the spiritual journey and the ultimate goal of union with God.

Sufism, with its deep roots in Islamic spirituality, offers a rich and multifaceted path to divine union. The origins of Sufism, emerging from the early Islamic community, reflect a profound desire to go beyond the outward forms of religion and seek a direct, personal experience of God. Through its diverse practices, Sufi orders, and the lives of its notable mystics, Sufism has provided countless seekers with a means to purify the soul, cultivate divine love, and experience the presence of God in every aspect of life.

The journey of Sufism is one of transformation, where the seeker moves through the stages of *fana* and *baqa*, transcending the self and realizing the unity of all existence in God. This journey is not only a personal one but also a communal one, as Sufi orders have played a crucial role in nurturing and guiding spiritual seekers throughout history.

It is clear that Sufism remains a vibrant and dynamic force within the Islamic world and beyond, offering timeless wisdom and practices that continue to inspire those who seek to deepen their relationship with the Divine. The teachings of Sufism remind us that the path to God is not a solitary one but a journey that is enriched by the love, guidance, and companionship of fellow seekers.

**Taoist Mysticism**

# Chapter 6: Taoist Mysticism

## Section 1: Foundational Texts

Taoist mysticism, with its profound emphasis on harmony with the natural world and the inner cultivation of spiritual wisdom, is deeply rooted in the foundational texts of Taoism. These texts, written over two millennia ago, continue to serve as the bedrock of Taoist thought and practice, offering insights into the nature of existence, the path to spiritual enlightenment, and the ultimate goal of unity with the Tao.

The most seminal text in Taoist mysticism is the *Tao Te Ching*, attributed to the sage Laozi, who is believed to have lived in the 6th century BCE. The *Tao Te Ching*, often translated as "The Book of the Way and Its Virtue," is a concise yet profound work consisting of 81 chapters, each offering poetic reflections on the nature of the Tao and the principles of living in harmony with it. The Tao, often described as the ineffable, underlying force that flows through all things, is both the source and the sustainer of the universe. Laozi's teachings emphasize the importance of aligning oneself with the Tao through simplicity, humility, and non-action (*wu wei*), a state of effortless action that arises when one is in perfect harmony with the natural order. The *Tao Te Ching* is not just a philosophical treatise but a mystical guide, inviting readers to contemplate the mysteries of existence and to cultivate an inner stillness that allows the Tao to manifest through them.

Another foundational text of Taoist mysticism is the *Zhuangzi*, attributed to the sage Zhuang Zhou, who lived during the 4th century BCE. The *Zhuangzi* is a collection of stories, parables, and philosophical musings that explore the nature of reality, the limitations of human knowledge, and the freedom that comes from living in accordance with the Tao. Unlike the more didactic style of the *Tao Te Ching*, the *Zhuangzi* is characterized by its playful and paradoxical tone, often using humor and irony to convey deep spiritual truths. One of the central themes of the *Zhuangzi* is the idea of *ziran* (naturalness or spontaneity), which suggests that true wisdom and spiritual freedom come from embracing the flow of life without attachment or resistance. The *Zhuangzi* challenges readers to let go of conventional thinking and to experience the world from a perspective that transcends dualistic distinctions, such as life and death, good and bad, or self and other.

The *Liezi*, attributed to the semi-legendary figure Lie Yukou, is another important text in Taoist mysticism. The *Liezi* shares many similarities with the *Zhuangzi*, both in style and content, and is often considered part of the same philosophical tradition. The *Liezi* is known for its emphasis on the relativity of human experience and the importance of cultivating inner detachment. It presents a vision of the universe as a dynamic, ever-changing process, where the wise person is one who can adapt to the ebb and flow of life without being caught up in the illusions of permanence or ego. The *Liezi* also contains discussions on the nature of dreams, the limits of human knowledge, and the concept of immortality, reflecting the text's deep engagement with the mysteries of existence.

In addition to these philosophical texts, Taoist mysticism is also grounded in a rich body of esoteric writings known as the *Daozang*, or Taoist Canon. The *Daozang* is a vast collection of scriptures, rituals, and commentaries that encompass a wide range of Taoist teachings and practices, including alchemy, meditation, divination, and cosmology.

Compiled over several centuries, the *Daozang* reflects the diversity of Taoist thought and its integration of various spiritual and mystical traditions. Among the most influential texts in the *Daozang* are the *Huangdi Neijing* (Yellow Emperor's Inner Classic), a foundational work on Taoist medicine and inner alchemy, and the *Wuzhen Pian* (Awakening to Reality), a key text in the study of Taoist alchemical practices.

The foundational texts of Taoist mysticism, while diverse in style and content, all share a common focus on the cultivation of harmony with the Tao and the realization of one's true nature. These texts serve as guides for those who seek to transcend the limitations of the ego and to experience the world in its fullness and interconnectedness. Through the study and contemplation of these works, practitioners of Taoism are invited to embark on a journey of inner transformation, where the boundaries between self and other, human and divine, begin to dissolve, revealing the underlying unity of all existence.

## Section 2: Taoist Concepts

At the heart of Taoist mysticism lies a rich array of concepts that shape its understanding of the universe, the self, and the path to spiritual enlightenment. These concepts, deeply rooted in the foundational texts of Taoism, offer profound insights into the nature of reality and the ways in which individuals can align themselves with the Tao.

One of the central concepts in Taoist thought is the Tao itself. The Tao, often translated as "the Way," is the ultimate, ineffable principle that underlies and unites all things. It is both the source of creation and the force that sustains the universe, transcending all dualities and distinctions. The Tao is beyond human comprehension, yet it is present in every aspect of life, from the vastness of the cosmos to the smallest grain of sand. In Taoist mysticism, the goal is to align oneself with the Tao, to live in harmony with its flow, and to cultivate a deep sense of unity with the natural world. This alignment is achieved not through force or willpower, but through *wu wei*, the practice of non-action or effortless action, where one acts in accordance with the natural order without striving or resistance.

Another key concept in Taoist mysticism is *yin* and *yang*, the complementary forces that represent the dualities inherent in the universe. *Yin* is associated with qualities such as darkness, passivity, and receptivity, while *yang* represents light, activity, and assertiveness. In Taoist thought, *yin* and *yang* are not opposing forces but are interdependent and constantly in flux, creating the dynamic balance that sustains the natural world. The interplay of *yin* and *yang* is seen in all aspects of life, from the cycles of day and night to the rhythms of the human body. Taoist mysticism teaches that spiritual wisdom comes from understanding and embracing the balance of *yin* and *yang*, allowing these forces to harmonize within oneself and the world.

*Qi* (or *chi*), often translated as "life force" or "vital energy," is another fundamental concept in Taoist mysticism. *Qi* is the energy that flows through all living things, connecting the individual to the universe. In Taoist practice, the cultivation and harmonization of *qi* are essential for physical health, spiritual well-being, and longevity. Through practices such as breath control, meditation, and Tai Chi, practitioners learn to regulate the flow of *qi* within their bodies, enhancing their vitality and deepening their connection to the Tao. The concept of *qi* underscores the Taoist belief in the interconnectedness of all life, where the health and balance of the individual are intimately tied to the greater harmony of the cosmos.

Taoist mysticism also places a strong emphasis on the concept of *ziran*, often translated as "naturalness" or "spontaneity." *Ziran* refers to the state of being that arises when one is in perfect harmony with the Tao, acting naturally and effortlessly in accordance with one's true nature. It is the state of authenticity and simplicity, where the individual is free from the constraints of social conditioning, ego, and artificial desires. In Taoist thought, *ziran* is the ideal state of being, where one lives in harmony with the rhythms of the natural world, embodying the qualities of humility, flexibility, and openness. The cultivation of *ziran* is seen as a path to spiritual enlightenment, where the individual becomes a reflection of the Tao's boundless creativity and wisdom.

Another important concept in Taoist mysticism is *wu*, often translated as "emptiness" or "nothingness." *Wu* is not merely the absence of something, but the fertile void from which all things arise. In Taoist thought, *wu* represents the potentiality of the universe, the source from which the Tao manifests. It is the space of infinite possibilities, where creation and transformation occur. The concept of *wu* is closely related to the practice of *wu wei*, where one embraces the emptiness and stillness within, allowing the natural flow of the Tao to guide one's actions. Taoist mysticism teaches that by cultivating an awareness of *wu*, individuals can tap into the creative power of the Tao, experiencing the fullness of life in its most essential form.

These Taoist concepts, each rich with meaning and depth, form the foundation of Taoist mysticism. They offer a framework for understanding the universe and one's place within it, guiding practitioners on a path of inner cultivation and harmony with the Tao. Through the exploration and embodiment of these concepts, individuals can transcend the limitations of the ego, experiencing the world as an interconnected, dynamic whole, where the boundaries between self and other, life and death, dissolve into the eternal flow of the Tao.

## Section 3: Alchemy and Immortality

Taoist mysticism encompasses a rich tradition of alchemy, which is not merely the pursuit of material transformation but, more importantly, a path to spiritual immortality. Taoist alchemy is divided into two main branches: external alchemy (*waidan*) and internal alchemy (*neidan*), both of which aim to achieve harmony with the Tao and attain eternal life, though their methods and focus differ.

External alchemy, or *waidan*, is the older of the two practices and involves the preparation of elixirs from minerals, herbs, and other natural substances. Practitioners of *waidan* sought to create the "elixir of immortality," a substance believed to grant physical longevity or even eternal life. The process of preparing these elixirs was highly ritualized and symbolically rich, reflecting the belief that the transformation of physical substances mirrored the transformation of the spirit. Although *waidan* has largely fallen out of favor due to the dangers associated with consuming these elixirs—many of which contained toxic substances—its symbolic significance endures in Taoist thought as a metaphor for the spiritual journey.

Internal alchemy, or *neidan*, emerged as a response to the limitations of *waidan* and represents a more introspective and spiritual approach to achieving immortality. *Neidan* focuses on the cultivation of the body, mind, and spirit through meditation, breath control, and the harmonization of internal energies. The goal of *neidan* is to refine the practitioner's vital energies—*jing* (essence), *qi* (life force), and *shen* (spirit)—and to transform them into pure spiritual energy. This process is often described as the "inner elixir," which, unlike the physical elixirs of *waidan*, is cultivated within the body and leads to spiritual immortality.

The practice of *neidan* is deeply rooted in the Taoist understanding of the human body as a microcosm of the universe. In this view, the body contains a network of energy channels (*meridians*) and centers (*dantian*) where vital energies are stored and transformed. Through disciplined practice, the internal alchemist seeks to balance and circulate these energies, purifying the body and mind and ultimately achieving a state of oneness with the Tao. This process is often depicted in Taoist texts as a journey of spiritual ascent, where the practitioner moves from the gross, material aspects of existence to the subtle, ethereal realms of pure spirit.

Immortality in Taoist mysticism is not simply about extending physical life but about transcending the limitations of the material world and achieving a state of eternal harmony with the Tao. The concept of immortality (*xian*) in Taoism is often portrayed as the transformation of the individual into an immortal being, free from the cycles of birth, death, and rebirth. These immortals, or *xian*, are believed to dwell in the celestial realms, having attained a perfect state of spiritual purity and union with the Tao.

The pursuit of immortality through *neidan* involves not only the cultivation of internal energies but also the cultivation of virtues such as humility, compassion, and simplicity. In this sense, Taoist alchemy is as much a moral and ethical practice as it is a physical and spiritual one. The true alchemist, in Taoist thought, is one who has mastered the art of living in harmony with the Tao, achieving a state of inner balance and peace that transcends the physical realm.

Taoist alchemy, with its profound focus on internal transformation and the pursuit of spiritual immortality, remains a central aspect of Taoist mysticism. It offers a pathway to deep spiritual insight and an understanding of the interconnectedness of all things, guiding practitioners toward the ultimate goal of unity with the Tao.

### Section 4: Philosophical vs. Religious Taoism

Taoism is a complex and multifaceted tradition, often divided into two primary strands: Philosophical Taoism and Religious Taoism. While these two forms of Taoism share common roots in the foundational texts and concepts, they differ significantly in their focus, practices, and expressions of the Taoist path.

Philosophical Taoism, also known as *Daojia*, is rooted in the teachings of Laozi and Zhuangzi, particularly as expressed in the *Tao Te Ching* and the *Zhuangzi*. This strand of Taoism emphasizes living in harmony with the Tao, the natural order of the universe, and cultivating virtues such as simplicity, humility, and spontaneity. Philosophical Taoism is often characterized by its focus on individual wisdom, ethical living, and the cultivation of inner peace through non-action (*wu wei*). It advocates a life of simplicity and detachment, encouraging practitioners to align themselves with the flow of nature and to avoid the artificial constructs of society that lead to discord and suffering.

Philosophical Taoism is primarily concerned with the metaphysical and ethical dimensions of the Tao. It offers a framework for understanding the nature of reality and the self, emphasizing the importance of intuition, flexibility, and the acceptance of life's inherent contradictions. The teachings of Philosophical Taoism are often seen as a guide for personal cultivation, where the individual seeks to attain harmony with the Tao through contemplation, meditation, and living in accordance with the principles of naturalness (*ziran*) and non-attachment.

In contrast, Religious Taoism, or *Daojiao*, represents the organized, ritualistic, and communal aspects of Taoism. This strand of Taoism developed over centuries, incorporating elements of Chinese folk religion, ancestor worship, and various esoteric practices. Religious Taoism is characterized by its pantheon of deities, rituals, and ceremonies designed to communicate with the divine and ensure the well-being of individuals and communities. Temples, priests, and religious orders play a central role in Religious Taoism, offering a structured approach to spiritual practice that includes rites of passage, healing rituals, and the worship of gods and immortals.

Religious Taoism also encompasses a wide range of practices aimed at achieving physical health, longevity, and spiritual immortality. These include alchemy, divination, astrology, and the cultivation of *qi* through martial arts, meditation, and breathing exercises. Religious Taoism places a strong emphasis on the interconnection between the material and spiritual worlds, viewing the physical body as a vessel that can be refined and perfected through disciplined practice. The rituals and ceremonies of Religious Taoism often seek to balance cosmic forces, appease spirits, and harmonize the environment, reflecting a deep concern for the welfare of both the individual and the community.

Despite their differences, Philosophical and Religious Taoism are not mutually exclusive. In fact, many Taoist practitioners and communities integrate aspects of both strands, drawing on the wisdom of the *Tao Te Ching* and the *Zhuangzi* while also participating in religious rituals and seeking the guidance of Taoist priests. The relationship between these two forms of Taoism is complex and dynamic, with each enriching the other in various ways.

Philosophical Taoism provides the metaphysical foundation and ethical principles that underpin Taoist thought, while Religious Taoism offers a practical, communal framework for living out these principles in everyday life. Together, they form a comprehensive spiritual tradition that addresses both the inner and outer dimensions of human existence, guiding practitioners toward a life of harmony, balance, and unity with the Tao.

## Section 5: Yin and Yang Balance

The concept of *yin* and *yang* is one of the most fundamental and iconic aspects of Taoist thought, symbolizing the dynamic balance of opposing forces that underlies the entire universe. In Taoist mysticism, the harmonious interplay of *yin* and *yang* is essential for understanding the nature of reality, achieving inner balance, and living in accordance with the Tao.

*Yin* and *yang* are not merely opposites; they are complementary forces that exist in a state of constant interaction and transformation. *Yin* is associated with qualities such as darkness, passivity, receptivity, and the feminine, while *yang* represents light, activity, assertiveness, and the masculine. Together, they create the duality that is evident in all aspects of life: night and day, winter and summer, stillness and movement, and so on. However, in Taoist thought, *yin* and *yang* are not static or mutually exclusive; each contains the seed of the other, symbolized by the familiar *taijitu* (yin-yang symbol), where a dot of *yin* exists within *yang* and vice versa.

The balance of *yin* and *yang* is seen as essential for maintaining harmony in both the natural world and the human body. In Taoist practices, achieving this balance is key to physical health, emotional well-being, and spiritual enlightenment. For instance, in Traditional Chinese Medicine (TCM), which is deeply influenced by Taoist philosophy, the balance of *yin* and *yang* within the body is crucial for preventing illness and maintaining vitality. Techniques such as acupuncture, herbal medicine, and qigong are used to harmonize these forces and restore balance when it is disrupted.

In the realm of spiritual practice, *yin* and *yang* balance is also reflected in the Taoist approach to meditation, martial arts, and alchemy. Taoist meditation often involves cultivating stillness (*yin*) and energy (*yang*) within the body, leading to a state of inner harmony and alignment with the Tao. Similarly, Taoist martial arts, such as Tai Chi, emphasize the fluid interchange of *yin* and *yang* energies, promoting both physical and spiritual balance.

On a broader level, the concept of *yin* and *yang* serves as a reminder of the interconnectedness of all things and the importance of embracing both the light and dark aspects of life. In Taoist mysticism, the path to enlightenment involves recognizing and harmonizing the *yin* and *yang* within oneself and the world, achieving a state of equilibrium that reflects the natural order of the cosmos.

Taoist mysticism, with its deep emphasis on harmony, balance, and the pursuit of spiritual immortality, offers a profound and holistic approach to understanding the nature of existence and the path to enlightenment. Through its foundational texts, core concepts, and diverse practices, Taoism guides practitioners toward a life of simplicity, spontaneity, and unity with the Tao.

The teachings of Taoism remind us that the journey to spiritual wisdom is not one of force or struggle but of aligning ourselves with the natural rhythms of the universe. Whether through the cultivation of *qi*, the practice of internal alchemy, or the pursuit of balance between *yin* and *yang*, Taoist mysticism offers timeless wisdom for those seeking to live in harmony with the world around them and the deeper currents of life itself.

By now it is clear that Taoist mysticism is not just a philosophy or religion but a way of being—one that encourages us to embrace the flow of life, to cultivate inner stillness, and to find our place within the ever-changing dance of existence. In doing so, we open ourselves to the boundless possibilities of the Tao, discovering the profound unity that underlies all things.

**Gnostic Mysticism**

# Chapter 7: Gnostic Mysticism

## Section 1: Gnostic Beliefs

Gnosticism represents one of the most enigmatic and esoteric strands of early Christian mysticism, characterized by its emphasis on hidden knowledge (*gnosis*) as the key to spiritual liberation. The term "Gnosticism" encompasses a diverse array of beliefs and practices that emerged in the early centuries of the Common Era, primarily within the context of the early Christian and Jewish communities. Central to Gnostic thought is the belief that the material world is a flawed or even evil creation, and that true salvation lies in transcending the physical realm to return to the divine source.

At the heart of Gnostic belief is the concept of dualism, particularly the duality between the material and spiritual worlds. Gnostics often viewed the material world as a place of darkness and ignorance, created by a lesser divine being known as the Demiurge. This Demiurge, often identified with the God of the Hebrew Bible, was seen as a misguided or malevolent figure who entrapped souls in the physical realm. In contrast, the true God, or the *Pleroma* (the fullness of the divine), was believed to reside in a higher, transcendent realm of pure light and spirit.

Gnostics believed that within each human being resides a divine spark, a fragment of the *Pleroma*, which has become imprisoned in the material world. The purpose of human life, according to Gnostic thought, is to awaken to this divine spark and to seek *gnosis*—a deep, experiential knowledge of the divine. *Gnosis* is not merely intellectual understanding but a transformative, mystical insight that reveals the true nature of the self and the universe.

Through *gnosis*, the soul can transcend the limitations of the material world and return to the divine source from which it originated.

The journey toward *gnosis* often involved a process of inner purification and spiritual ascent. Gnostics practiced various forms of meditation, contemplation, and asceticism to detach themselves from the illusions and desires of the physical world. They also engaged in rituals and sacraments, such as baptism and the Eucharist, which were reinterpreted as symbolic acts of spiritual awakening and liberation. For Gnostics, the ultimate goal was to achieve *gnosis* and to ascend through the various levels of the cosmos, eventually reuniting with the divine *Pleroma*.

Another key belief in Gnostic mysticism is the idea of the divine feminine, often personified as Sophia, the goddess of wisdom. In many Gnostic cosmologies, Sophia plays a central role in the creation of the material world and the redemption of humanity. According to these narratives, Sophia, in her desire to know the true God, descended from the *Pleroma* and became trapped in the material world, inadvertently giving birth to the Demiurge. Her fall from the divine realm is mirrored in the fall of human souls into the material world. However, Sophia also serves as the guide and redeemer of humanity, leading souls back to the divine through the revelation of *gnosis*. The figure of Sophia highlights the Gnostic emphasis on wisdom and inner knowledge as the path to spiritual liberation.

Gnostic texts, such as those found in the Nag Hammadi library, often depict a complex cosmology with multiple layers of divine beings, archons (rulers of the material world), and aeons (emanations of the divine). These texts, including the *Gospel of Thomas*, the *Gospel of Philip*, and the *Apocryphon of John*, present a vision of the cosmos as a battleground between the forces of light and darkness, spirit and matter. In this cosmic struggle, the Gnostic seeker is called to rise above the material plane and to seek communion with the divine.

Gnostic beliefs also include a radical reinterpretation of traditional religious narratives. For example, the story of the Fall in the Garden of Eden is often seen in Gnostic thought as a positive event, where the serpent (representing Sophia or the force of *gnosis*) offers Adam and Eve the knowledge of good and evil, thereby awakening them to their true divine nature. This inversion of traditional interpretations reflects the Gnostic view that conventional religious teachings often serve to keep souls in ignorance, rather than leading them to spiritual enlightenment.

In summary, Gnostic mysticism is defined by its emphasis on hidden knowledge, dualism, and the quest for spiritual liberation. It presents a worldview that is both mystical and radical, challenging the materialist assumptions of the world and offering a path to transcendence through inner knowledge and divine wisdom. The beliefs of Gnosticism have left a lasting impact on the history of mysticism and continue to inspire those who seek a deeper understanding of the mysteries of existence.

## Section 2: Historical Context

Gnosticism emerged during a tumultuous period in the history of the ancient Mediterranean world, a time marked by significant cultural, religious, and political changes. The early centuries of the Common Era, particularly from the 1st to the 4th century CE, saw the rise of various religious movements, including early Christianity, Judaism, and the mystery religions of the Greco-Roman world. It was within this complex and diverse religious landscape that Gnosticism took shape, drawing on influences from multiple traditions and developing its unique mystical worldview.

The origins of Gnosticism are difficult to trace with precision, as it was not a single, unified movement but rather a collection of related sects and schools of thought. Some scholars believe that Gnosticism has roots in pre-Christian Jewish mysticism, particularly in the apocalyptic and esoteric traditions of Second Temple Judaism. Elements of Gnostic thought, such as the belief in a hidden, transcendent God and the concept of divine wisdom (Sophia), can be found in Jewish mystical texts like the *Book of Enoch* and the *Wisdom of Solomon*. These texts, which explore themes of divine revelation, spiritual ascent, and the cosmic struggle between good and evil, provided a fertile ground for the development of Gnostic ideas.

Gnosticism also drew heavily on the religious and philosophical currents of the Hellenistic world. The spread of Greek culture and thought following the conquests of Alexander the Great brought about a blending of Eastern and Western traditions, creating a cosmopolitan intellectual environment in which Gnostic ideas could flourish. Platonic philosophy, with its emphasis on the distinction between the material and spiritual realms, had a profound influence on Gnostic thought. The Platonic concept of the *Demiurge*, a lesser god who creates the material world, closely parallels the Gnostic idea of the Demiurge as a flawed or malevolent creator. Additionally, the Platonic notion of the soul's ascent from the material world to the realm of pure forms is echoed in the Gnostic belief in the soul's journey toward the divine *Pleroma*.

The early Christian movement also played a crucial role in the development of Gnosticism. As Christianity spread throughout the Roman Empire, it encountered a wide variety of religious and philosophical traditions, leading to the formation of diverse interpretations of the Christian message. Some early Christians, influenced by Gnostic ideas, began to reinterpret the teachings of Jesus in a mystical and esoteric manner. These Gnostic Christians emphasized the hidden, inner meaning of Jesus' teachings and sought to uncover the *gnosis* that would lead to spiritual liberation. Gnostic texts such as the *Gospel of Thomas* and the *Gospel of Mary* present a vision of Jesus as a divine teacher who imparts secret knowledge to his disciples, guiding them on the path to enlightenment.

The spread of Gnosticism in the early Christian period was met with significant resistance from orthodox Christian authorities. The early Church Fathers, including figures like Irenaeus, Tertullian, and Hippolytus, condemned Gnosticism as heretical and sought to suppress its teachings. In his work *Against Heresies*, Irenaeus argued that Gnostic teachings were a perversion of the true Christian faith, accusing Gnostics of distorting the message of the Gospel and leading believers astray. The Church Fathers were particularly concerned with the Gnostic rejection of the material world and the traditional understanding of God as the creator of the universe. They saw Gnosticism as a dangerous threat to the unity and purity of the Christian faith, leading to the eventual marginalization and decline of Gnostic sects within the broader Christian community.

Despite this suppression, Gnostic ideas continued to influence Christian mysticism and theology in subtle ways. Elements of Gnostic thought can be seen in the writings of later Christian mystics, such as the emphasis on inner knowledge, the soul's ascent to God, and the quest for spiritual perfection. Moreover, Gnosticism found new life in various esoteric and mystical traditions throughout history, including the Hermeticism of the Renaissance, the Kabbalah of Jewish mysticism, and the modern New Age movement.

The discovery of the Nag Hammadi library in 1945, a collection of Gnostic texts buried in the Egyptian desert, sparked renewed interest in Gnosticism and its place in the history of early Christianity. These texts, many of which had been lost or suppressed for centuries, provided scholars with invaluable insights into the beliefs, practices, and diversity of Gnostic thought. The Nag Hammadi texts revealed the richness and complexity of Gnostic mysticism, challenging the simplistic portrayals of Gnosticism as a monolithic or purely heretical movement.

In conclusion, the historical context of Gnostic mysticism is one of dynamic interaction between various religious and philosophical traditions. Gnosticism emerged as a response to the spiritual and intellectual challenges of its time, offering a radical alternative to the dominant religious narratives. Its legacy, though often obscured or marginalized, continues to resonate in the mystical and esoteric traditions of the modern world.

### Section 3: Key Texts

The rich and complex tradition of Gnostic mysticism is captured in a variety of key texts, many of which were hidden or suppressed for centuries. These writings, often composed in the early centuries of the Common Era, provide profound insights into the beliefs, cosmology, and spiritual practices of Gnostic communities. The discovery of the Nag Hammadi library in 1945 brought many of these texts to light, allowing scholars and spiritual seekers alike to explore the depths of Gnostic thought.

One of the most significant Gnostic texts is the *Gospel of Thomas*, a collection of 114 sayings attributed to Jesus. Unlike the canonical Gospels, which focus on the life and teachings of Jesus within a narrative framework, the *Gospel of Thomas* presents Jesus' sayings as enigmatic and mystical aphorisms. Many of these sayings emphasize the importance of self-knowledge and inner revelation as the path to divine truth. For example, the famous saying, "If you bring forth what is within you, what you have will save you; if you do not bring forth what is within you, what you do not have will destroy you," encapsulates the Gnostic emphasis on inner transformation and the discovery of the divine spark within. The *Gospel of Thomas* challenges conventional religious interpretations, inviting readers to seek a deeper, more personal understanding of spiritual truths.

Another key text is the *Apocryphon of John*, a cosmological work that provides a detailed account of the Gnostic creation myth. The *Apocryphon of John* describes the origin of the material world as a flawed creation of the Demiurge, a lesser god who is ignorant of the true divine realm. This text also introduces the figure of Sophia, the divine wisdom who plays a central role in the Gnostic narrative of fall and redemption. Sophia's descent into the material world and her eventual redemption mirror the Gnostic soul's journey from ignorance to enlightenment. The *Apocryphon of John* offers a profound exploration of the nature of the cosmos, the role of the divine feminine, and the path to spiritual liberation.

The *Gospel of Philip* is another important Gnostic text, known for its exploration of the sacraments and their mystical significance. Unlike the orthodox Christian interpretation of the sacraments as outward rituals, the *Gospel of Philip* presents them as symbolic acts that reveal deeper spiritual truths. For example, the sacrament of the bridal chamber, a central theme in the *Gospel of Philip*, is interpreted as a mystical union between the soul and the divine, representing the ultimate goal of *gnosis*. The *Gospel of Philip* also emphasizes the importance of *gnosis* as the means of transcending the material world and achieving spiritual immortality.

The *Pistis Sophia* is another major Gnostic text, particularly within the tradition of the Sethian Gnostics. This text is a lengthy and complex dialogue between Jesus and his disciples, focusing on the figure of Sophia and her role in the cosmic drama of redemption. The *Pistis Sophia* provides a detailed account of the soul's journey through various spiritual realms, offering insight into the Gnostic understanding of salvation and the afterlife. The text is notable for its rich symbolism and its emphasis on the struggle between light and darkness, spirit and matter.

These key texts, along with others found in the Nag Hammadi library, form the core of Gnostic literature. They offer a window into the mystical and esoteric world of Gnosticism, revealing the depth of its spiritual insights and the diversity of its teachings. For those interested in exploring Gnostic mysticism, these texts provide a valuable foundation for understanding the beliefs and practices of this ancient tradition.

**Section 4: Influence and Legacy**

The influence and legacy of Gnostic mysticism extend far beyond its early roots in the ancient Mediterranean world. Despite the suppression of Gnostic ideas by orthodox Christian authorities, Gnosticism has left an indelible mark on the history of Western spirituality, influencing a wide range of religious and philosophical traditions.

One of the most significant areas of Gnostic influence is in early Christian mysticism. While many Church Fathers denounced Gnosticism as heretical, certain elements of Gnostic thought found their way into the writings of later Christian mystics. The emphasis on inner knowledge, the soul's ascent to God, and the experience of divine union are themes that resonate strongly in the works of mystics such as St. Augustine, Meister Eckhart, and St. John of the Cross. These mystics, while adhering to orthodox Christian theology, often explored concepts that echoed Gnostic ideas, such as the transformative power of *gnosis* and the mystical journey toward spiritual enlightenment.

Gnosticism also had a profound impact on the development of esoteric traditions in the Middle Ages and the Renaissance. The resurgence of interest in Hermeticism, Kabbalah, and alchemy during this period was deeply influenced by Gnostic ideas. The Hermetic texts, which share many similarities with Gnostic thought, were rediscovered and translated during the Renaissance, leading to a revival of interest in mystical and esoteric knowledge. The concept of hidden wisdom, central to Gnosticism, became a key theme in these traditions, influencing the work of philosophers, alchemists, and mystics who sought to uncover the secrets of the cosmos and the human soul.

The legacy of Gnosticism can also be seen in the rise of various spiritual movements and sects throughout history. The Cathars, a medieval Christian sect in southern France, embraced many Gnostic beliefs, including the dualistic view of the world and the rejection of the material as evil. The Cathars were eventually persecuted and eradicated by the Catholic Church, but their teachings continued to influence later spiritual movements, including the Albigensian Crusade and the Waldensians.

In modern times, Gnosticism has experienced a revival, particularly within the context of the New Age movement and contemporary spirituality. The rediscovery of the Nag Hammadi texts in the mid-20th century sparked renewed interest in Gnostic thought, leading to the formation of new Gnostic churches and the publication of numerous books on Gnostic spirituality. Gnostic themes of inner knowledge, the divine feminine, and the quest for spiritual awakening have resonated with many contemporary seekers who are drawn to alternative spiritual paths.

The legacy of Gnosticism is also evident in popular culture, where Gnostic themes have been explored in literature, film, and art. Works such as Philip K. Dick's *VALIS* trilogy, the films of The Matrix trilogy, and the writings of Carl Jung all draw on Gnostic ideas, reflecting the enduring relevance of Gnostic mysticism in the modern world.

The influence and legacy of Gnosticism are vast and far-reaching, touching upon many aspects of Western spirituality and culture. Despite the challenges it faced in its early history, Gnosticism has continued to inspire and provoke thought, offering a unique perspective on the nature of reality, the soul, and the path to spiritual liberation.

## Section 5: Gnosticism's Modern Relevance

Gnosticism, with its emphasis on inner knowledge and spiritual awakening, has found renewed relevance in the modern world. In an era marked by existential uncertainty, materialism, and a search for deeper meaning, Gnostic ideas offer a path to personal and spiritual fulfillment that resonates with contemporary seekers.

One of the reasons for Gnosticism's modern relevance is its focus on the individual's direct experience of the divine. In contrast to traditional religious structures that emphasize external authority and dogma, Gnosticism encourages a personal, experiential relationship with the divine, where *gnosis*—inner knowledge—takes precedence over belief. This emphasis on personal spirituality appeals to those who are disillusioned with institutional religion and are seeking a more direct and authentic spiritual experience.

Gnosticism's dualistic worldview, which distinguishes between the material and spiritual realms, also resonates with modern concerns about the environment, technology, and the alienation of the self in a rapidly changing world. The Gnostic critique of the material world as a place of darkness and ignorance can be seen as a metaphor for the challenges of contemporary life, where individuals often feel disconnected from their true selves and the natural world. The Gnostic call to awaken to the divine spark within and to transcend the material world offers a way of addressing these challenges, encouraging a return to a more spiritual and harmonious way of living.

The resurgence of interest in the divine feminine is another aspect of Gnosticism that has found modern relevance. The figure of Sophia, the goddess of wisdom, represents the rediscovery of the feminine aspect of the divine, which has often been marginalized or suppressed in patriarchal religious traditions. In contemporary spirituality, the embrace of the divine feminine is seen as a way of healing the wounds of gender inequality and restoring balance to the spiritual and social order.

Moreover, Gnosticism's emphasis on hidden knowledge and the uncovering of spiritual truths has influenced the New Age movement and various esoteric traditions. In a world where information is abundant but true wisdom is scarce, the Gnostic pursuit of *gnosis*—deep, transformative knowledge—offers a path to spiritual enlightenment that goes beyond surface-level understanding. This pursuit of hidden wisdom, whether through meditation, study, or inner reflection, is a key aspect of modern Gnostic practice.

Gnosticism's modern relevance lies in its ability to address the spiritual needs and concerns of contemporary life. Its emphasis on personal spirituality, the divine feminine, and the quest for hidden knowledge offers a rich and meaningful path for those seeking to navigate the complexities of the modern world and to find a deeper connection with the divine.

Gnostic mysticism continues to offer a unique and compelling perspective on the nature of existence. Through its key texts, such as the *Gospel of Thomas* and the *Apocryphon of John*, Gnosticism presents a vision of the world that challenges conventional religious narratives and invites seekers to embark on a journey of inner transformation.

The historical context of Gnosticism reveals its deep roots in the early Christian and Jewish traditions, as well as its interactions with the philosophical and religious currents of the Hellenistic world. Despite facing suppression by orthodox Christian authorities, Gnosticism has left a lasting legacy, influencing a wide range of mystical, esoteric, and philosophical traditions throughout history.

In the modern world, Gnosticism's relevance is perhaps more pronounced than ever. Its focus on personal spirituality, the divine feminine, and the pursuit of inner knowledge resonates with contemporary seekers who are looking for a deeper, more authentic connection to the divine. Gnosticism offers timeless wisdom and a path to spiritual liberation that continues to inspire and guide those on the mystical journey.

## Lesser-Known Mystical Traditions

## Chapter 8: Lesser-Known Mystical Traditions

### Section 1: Shamanism

Shamanism is one of the oldest spiritual practices in the world, with roots that stretch back tens of thousands of years. It is a form of spirituality that centers on the shaman, a figure who serves as an intermediary between the physical world and the spiritual realms. Found in indigenous cultures across the globe—from the Americas to Siberia, Mongolia, and beyond—shamanism involves rituals, ceremonies, and practices designed to heal, guide, and connect individuals and communities with the spirit world.

**Key Concepts:**

- **Journeying:** Central to shamanic practice is the concept of journeying, where the shaman enters an altered state of consciousness to travel to the spirit world. Through this journey, the shaman communicates with spirits, ancestors, and other entities to gain wisdom, seek healing, or retrieve lost souls. This practice often involves the use of drumming, chanting, and sometimes plant medicine to induce the altered state.
- **Animal Spirits:** In many shamanic traditions, animals are seen as powerful spiritual guides. Shamans may call upon specific animal spirits for their protective, healing, or guiding powers. These spirits are often considered to be embodiments of certain qualities or attributes that can assist the shaman or the community.
- **The Shaman's Role:** Shamans are often viewed as healers, not just of the body, but of the mind and soul. They are responsible for maintaining balance within the community and the natural world. By acting as a bridge between the physical and spiritual realms, shamans help to

restore harmony and offer insight into the deeper aspects of existence.

## Section 2: The Mysticism of Indigenous African Religions

Indigenous African religions are rich with mystical traditions that are deeply intertwined with the cultural, social, and spiritual lives of the people. These traditions are often passed down through oral history and are practiced within a communal context, where rituals, ceremonies, and ancestor veneration play a central role. The mystical aspects of these religions offer a unique perspective on the interconnectedness of life, the power of the ancestors, and the living energy present in all elements of nature.

**Key Concepts:**

  - **The Power of Ancestors:** Ancestor veneration is a key component of many African spiritual traditions. Ancestors are seen as powerful spiritual beings who continue to play an active role in the lives of the living. They are revered, consulted, and honored through rituals and offerings, and their guidance is sought in matters ranging from health to social harmony.
  - **Living Energy in Natural Elements:** In many African traditions, natural elements—such as water, earth, fire, and air—are imbued with spiritual significance. Rivers, mountains, and trees, for example, are often considered sacred and are believed to be inhabited by spirits. The practice of honoring these natural elements reflects a deep reverence for the environment and the belief in the interconnectedness of all life.
  - **Ubuntu:** The concept of Ubuntu, often translated as "I am because we are," is a philosophical and spiritual

principle that emphasizes human interconnectedness and the importance of community. In the mystical context, Ubuntu reflects the belief that individual well-being is inherently linked to the well-being of others and the natural world. This principle is central to many African spiritual practices and is a guiding force in maintaining social and spiritual harmony.

## Section 3: Australian Aboriginal Dreamtime

Dreamtime is the cornerstone of the spiritual belief system of the Indigenous peoples of Australia. It represents the sacred era of creation, a time when ancestral spirits emerged from the earth to create the land, its features, and all living beings. Dreamtime is not just a historical event but a timeless, ongoing process that connects the past, present, and future. The stories, rituals, and art of Dreamtime are passed down through generations, preserving the spiritual laws and truths that guide Aboriginal life.

## Key Concepts:

- **Interconnectedness of All Beings:** Dreamtime teaches that all beings—humans, animals, plants, and even the land itself—are interconnected and share a common ancestry. This belief fosters a deep respect for the environment and a sense of responsibility for its care. The land is seen as a living entity, and the bonds between the land and its inhabitants are sacred.
- **Significance of Land and Totems:** Land is central to Aboriginal spirituality, and specific sites are considered sacred because they are believed to be the dwelling places of ancestral spirits. Totems, which can be animals, plants, or natural features, represent the spiritual connection

between individuals or groups and their ancestral beings. Totems serve as symbols of identity, protection, and guidance.

  - **Oral Tradition and Storytelling:** Dreamtime stories, passed down orally, are a vital means of conveying spiritual truths, laws, and moral lessons. These stories often describe the deeds of ancestral beings and explain the origins of the land, its features, and its inhabitants. Storytelling is a sacred practice that ensures the continuation of spiritual knowledge and cultural heritage.

### Section 4: Bon: Pre-Buddhist Mysticism of Tibet

Bon is the ancient spiritual tradition of Tibet, predating the arrival of Buddhism by several centuries. It is a rich and complex system that combines shamanistic, animistic, and mystical practices. Bon teaches that the natural world is alive with spirits and that these spirits can be communicated with through rituals and ceremonies. Although it shares some similarities with Tibetan Buddhism, Bon maintains its own unique cosmology, deities, and spiritual practices.

### Key Concepts:

  - **Rituals for Protection and Healing:** Bon rituals often involve elaborate ceremonies to appease spirits, protect against negative forces, and promote healing. These rituals are led by Bon shamans, who are skilled in invoking deities and spirits to aid in these processes. The use of mantras, offerings, and symbolic objects is central to these rituals.
  - **Spirits of Nature:** In Bon, nature is seen as being inhabited by a multitude of spirits, each with its own role and influence. Mountains, rivers, trees, and other natural features are considered sacred and are respected as the

abodes of these spirits. Communicating with and honoring these spirits is essential for maintaining harmony with the natural world.

- **Dzogchen:** Dzogchen, or the "Great Perfection," is a central practice in Bon that aims to help practitioners realize their true nature and achieve enlightenment. Dzogchen teachings focus on the direct experience of the primordial state of being, beyond dualistic concepts and the ordinary mind. Through meditation and contemplation, practitioners seek to uncover this innate purity and live in harmony with the universe.

## Section 5: Alchemical Traditions

Alchemy, often misunderstood as merely a quest to turn base metals into gold, is deeply mystical and symbolic, focusing on the transformation of the self. Alchemical traditions, found in various cultures including the Western, Islamic, and Chinese worlds, encompass both physical and spiritual practices aimed at achieving wisdom, enlightenment, and the perfection of the soul.

## Key Concepts:

- **The Philosopher's Stone:** In alchemical symbolism, the Philosopher's Stone represents the ultimate goal of the alchemist's work. It is not only a material substance that can transform lead into gold but also a metaphor for spiritual enlightenment and immortality. The search for the Philosopher's Stone is symbolic of the soul's journey toward perfection and union with the divine.
- **Individuation and Transformation:** Alchemy is often seen as a process of individuation, where the alchemist undergoes a series of inner transformations that mirror the outer work of transmutation. This process involves the

purification of the self, the integration of opposites, and the realization of the divine nature within.

- **Unity of Opposites:** Alchemy teaches that true wisdom and transformation come from the union of opposites—such as spirit and matter, masculine and feminine, light and dark. This concept is central to the alchemical tradition, where the reconciliation of these dualities leads to the creation of the "One Thing," a state of wholeness and unity.

## Section 6: The Mystical Aspect of Philosophical Taoism

Philosophical Taoism, rooted in the teachings of Laozi and Zhuangzi, offers profound insights into the nature of the universe and the path to living in harmony with the Tao. While often associated with ethical living and personal wisdom, Philosophical Taoism also carries a mystical dimension that emphasizes the importance of aligning oneself with the Tao—the fundamental principle that underlies all existence. It bridges the gap between thought and action, guiding practitioners toward a state of inner peace and unity with the Tao.

This mystical aspect of Philosophical Taoism provides a framework for understanding how the Tao manifests in the natural world and within the self, offering a path to spiritual enlightenment that is both grounded in philosophy and deeply experiential.

While Taoism is often divided into philosophical and religious strands, the mystical aspects of Philosophical Taoism offer profound insights into the nature of the universe and the path to spiritual enlightenment. Philosophical Taoism emphasizes living in harmony with the Tao, the fundamental principle that underlies all existence, and cultivating virtues such as simplicity, humility, and spontaneity.

**Key Concepts:**

- **Wu Wei (Effortless Action):** Central to Taoist mysticism is the concept of *wu wei*, which can be translated as "non-action" or "effortless action." *Wu wei* is the practice of aligning oneself so completely with the Tao that one's actions flow naturally and effortlessly, without force or struggle. It is about being in harmony with the rhythms of the universe, allowing the Tao to guide one's life.

- **Ziran (Spontaneity):** *Ziran* refers to the natural state of being, acting in accordance with one's true nature. In Taoist mysticism, spontaneity is not about impulsiveness but about being true to the essence of the Tao within oneself. It is the expression of authenticity and simplicity, free from the constraints of social conventions or artificial desires.

- **Pursuit of Longevity and Immortality:** Taoist mysticism also includes practices aimed at achieving longevity and immortality, not just in the physical sense but as a spiritual goal. This pursuit involves the cultivation of *qi* (vital energy) through meditation, breath control, and inner alchemy, with the aim of harmonizing body, mind, and spirit and aligning with the Tao.

**Section 7: Sikh Mysticism**

**Overview:** Sikhism, while known for its strong emphasis on social justice, equality, and community service, also has a profound mystical dimension. Sikh mysticism centers on the experience of the divine through meditation, devotional singing (Kirtan), and living according to the teachings of the Sikh Gurus. The ultimate goal is to realize the presence of

God within oneself and to live in constant remembrance of the divine.

**Key Concepts:**

- **Ik Onkar (One God):** The central tenet of Sikhism is the belief in *Ik Onkar*, the oneness of God. Sikh mysticism emphasizes the realization that this one God is present in all creation and within every individual. The experience of this divine unity is the essence of Sikh spiritual practice.
- **Naam (The Divine Name):** Meditation on the divine name, or *Naam*, is a key practice in Sikh mysticism. Through the repetition of God's name, Sikhs seek to purify their hearts and minds, draw closer to the divine, and experience spiritual bliss. *Naam* is seen as the means by which one can transcend the ego and merge with the divine.
- **The Inner Journey:** Sikh mysticism teaches that the true journey is an inner one, where the seeker moves beyond the distractions of the external world to discover the divine within. This journey involves self-discipline, humility, and devotion, as well as the guidance of the Guru, whose teachings illuminate the path to God.

These lesser-known mystical traditions showcase the rich diversity of spiritual practices around the world, it offers a deeper understanding of the universal human quest for connection with the divine. By exploring these traditions—Shamanism, Indigenous African Religions, Australian Aboriginal Dreamtime, Bon, Alchemical Traditions, Philosophical Taoism, and Sikh Mysticism—we gain insight into the many ways that different cultures have sought to understand and experience the mysteries of existence. Each tradition, with its unique practices and beliefs, contributes to the mosaic of human spirituality, offering valuable lessons for seekers on their journey toward enlightenment.

# Conclusion:

## Integrating Wisdom

In our modern world, where the pace of life is ever-accelerating and distractions are abundant, the ancient mystical wisdom of the past offers a grounding and transformative force. These teachings, which have been passed down through generations, carry timeless truths that remain as relevant today as they were millennia ago. Integrating this wisdom into contemporary life is not merely an act of preserving the past; it is a way of enriching our present and future, offering profound insights into the nature of existence, the self, and the universe.

Ancient mystical traditions, whether from the East or West, all share a common focus on inner transformation and spiritual awakening. These traditions teach us that true wisdom is not found in external achievements or material possessions, but in the cultivation of inner peace, compassion, and understanding. In a world often dominated by materialism and superficial values, the wisdom of the mystics invites us to turn inward, to seek a deeper connection with ourselves, others, and the divine.

One of the most valuable lessons from these mystical traditions is the concept of interconnectedness—the understanding that all beings, all things, are intrinsically linked. This perspective challenges the modern tendency toward individualism and isolation, reminding us that our well-being is intimately connected with the well-being of others and the natural world. By embracing this wisdom, we can foster a greater sense of empathy, cooperation, and stewardship, leading to a more harmonious and sustainable way of living.

The practice of mindfulness, now widely embraced in the West, is one example of how ancient mystical wisdom has been successfully integrated into contemporary life. Rooted in Buddhist and Taoist traditions, mindfulness encourages us to live in the present moment, fully aware of our thoughts, feelings, and surroundings. This practice not only reduces stress and anxiety but also enhances our ability to respond to life's challenges with clarity and equanimity. It exemplifies how the teachings of the mystics can be adapted to address the specific needs and challenges of our time.

Another important aspect of integrating mystical wisdom into modern life is the recognition of the spiritual dimension of existence. In a world that often prioritizes the material and tangible, the mystics remind us of the importance of nurturing the soul. Whether through meditation, prayer, or contemplation, these practices open us to experiences of transcendence, allowing us to connect with something greater than ourselves. This connection can provide a source of comfort, guidance, and inspiration, helping us navigate the complexities of life with a sense of purpose and meaning.

Furthermore, the mystics teach us about the power of simplicity and humility. In a culture that often celebrates excess and ego, the wisdom of the mystics calls us to live with less, to be content with what we have, and to approach life with a sense of reverence and gratitude. This shift in perspective can lead to a more fulfilling and balanced life, where we are not constantly striving for more but are instead cultivating a deeper appreciation for the present moment and the gifts it brings.

Integrating ancient mystical wisdom into contemporary life is not about retreating from the world or rejecting modern advancements. Rather, it is about bringing the insights of the past into dialogue with the present, creating a more holistic and enriched way of living. By doing so, we can draw on the best of both worlds—the wisdom of the ancients and the innovations of the modern age—to create a life that is both spiritually and materially fulfilling.

The ancient mystical traditions offer us a treasure trove of wisdom that, when integrated into our daily lives, can lead to greater inner peace, deeper connections, and a more meaningful existence. As we continue to navigate the complexities of the modern world, these teachings can serve as a guiding light, helping us to live with greater awareness, compassion, and understanding.

**The Universal Quest**

Throughout history, across cultures and continents, humanity has engaged in a universal quest: the search for deeper understanding, connection, and meaning. This quest, which lies at the heart of all mystical traditions, is driven by an innate desire to transcend the ordinary and to touch the divine. It is a journey that unites us all, regardless of our backgrounds, beliefs, or circumstances, reflecting the shared human experience of seeking something greater than ourselves.

The mystical traditions we have explored in this book—whether rooted in the East or West, ancient or modern—all speak to this universal quest. Despite their differences in language, symbolism, and practice, these traditions share a common goal: to awaken the human spirit to its true nature and to the profound mysteries of existence. This awakening is not simply an intellectual understanding but a transformative experience that changes the way we see ourselves, others, and the world.

One of the most striking aspects of this universal quest is the recognition of the divine within the self. Mystics across traditions have taught that the divine is not distant or separate, but is present within each of us. This realization is often described as a moment of enlightenment or union with the divine, where the boundaries between self and other, human and divine, dissolve. This experience of oneness is at the core of mystical practice and serves as a powerful reminder of the interconnectedness of all life.

The journey toward this realization is often described as a path—a series of steps, stages, or practices that lead the seeker closer to the divine. In Advaita Vedanta, this path involves the dissolution of the ego and the realization of the self as one with Brahman, the ultimate reality. In Sufism, it is the path of love, where the seeker's heart is purified through devotion and remembrance of God. In Kabbalah, it is the journey up the Tree of Life, where the seeker ascends through the mystical realms to reach the divine. Despite the different metaphors and frameworks, the essence of the journey remains the same: a process of inner transformation and spiritual awakening.

This universal quest is also reflected in the ethical teachings of the mystics, which emphasize the importance of love, compassion, and humility. These virtues are not just moral imperatives but are seen as essential qualities for those on the mystical path. By cultivating these virtues, the seeker becomes more attuned to the divine presence within and around them, creating a life that is in harmony with the divine will. This ethical dimension of mysticism highlights the inseparability of spiritual and moral development, where the realization of the divine is accompanied by a deepening of one's character and relationships.

The mystical quest is not limited to any one culture, religion, or time period—it is a timeless and universal journey that continues to inspire and guide people around the world. In our increasingly interconnected world, the mystical traditions offer a bridge between cultures, showing us that, despite our differences, we are all engaged in the same fundamental pursuit. This recognition of our shared humanity can foster greater understanding, tolerance, and peace, as we come to see that the barriers that divide us are illusory.

In the modern world, where materialism and rationalism often dominate, the mystical quest offers a counterbalance, reminding us of the importance of the spiritual dimension of life. It invites us to look beyond the surface of things, to question the assumptions of the material world, and to seek a deeper understanding of the mysteries of existence. This quest is not an escape from reality but a deeper engagement with it, where the seeker learns to see the divine in all things and to live in accordance with this vision.

As we conclude this exploration of mystical traditions, it is clear that the quest for deeper understanding and connection is a universal and timeless pursuit. It is a journey that unites us all, regardless of our differences, and that speaks to the deepest longings of the human heart. Whether through meditation, prayer, contemplation, or service, the mystical path offers a way to connect with the divine, to transform our lives, and to contribute to the greater good of humanity.

In the end, the mystical quest is not just about personal enlightenment but about the realization that we are all part of a greater whole—a vast, interconnected web of life that is sustained by the divine. By embarking on this journey, we contribute to the healing and transformation of the world, helping to create a future that is guided by wisdom, compassion, and love.

# Further Reading

For those who wish to delve deeper into the mystical traditions and concepts discussed in this book, the following resources offer a wealth of knowledge and insight:

1. **"The Tao Te Ching" by Lao Tzu** - A foundational text of Taoism, offering profound insights into the nature of the Tao and the principles of living in harmony with it.

2. **"The Upanishads"** - A collection of ancient Indian texts that explore the nature of reality, the self, and the ultimate truth, forming the philosophical basis of Advaita Vedanta.

3. **"The Zohar: The Book of Splendor" by Daniel C. Matt** - An accessible translation of one of the most important texts of Kabbalistic mysticism, exploring the mystical dimensions of the Torah.

4. **"The Essential Rumi" translated by Coleman Barks** - A collection of poems by the Sufi mystic Rumi, offering insights into the path of love, devotion, and spiritual union with the Divine.

5. **"The Gnostic Gospels" by Elaine Pagels** - A scholarly exploration of the Gnostic texts discovered at Nag Hammadi, shedding light on early Christian mysticism and its impact on Western spirituality.

6. **"The Tibetan Book of the Dead" translated by Robert A.F. Thurman** - A key text in Tibetan Buddhism and Bon, offering guidance on the journey of the soul after death and the practices for achieving liberation.

7. **"Alchemy: The Medieval Alchemists and Their Royal Art" by Johannes Fabricius** - An exploration of the mystical and symbolic aspects of alchemy, focusing on the quest for spiritual transformation.

8. **"Sikh Spiritual Practice: The Sound Way to God" by Siri Kirpal Kaur Khalsa** - An introduction to the mystical practices of Sikhism, including meditation, kirtan, and the inner journey toward divine union.

9. **"Shamanism: Archaic Techniques of Ecstasy" by Mircea Eliade** - A comprehensive study of shamanic practices across cultures, exploring the role of the shaman as a healer and mediator between the physical and spiritual worlds.

10. **"Dreamtime: Aboriginal Stories of the Creation" by A.W. Reed** - A collection of stories from Australian Aboriginal mythology, offering insights into the spiritual beliefs and practices of the Dreamtime.

These books provide a deeper exploration of the mystical traditions, practices, and philosophies discussed in this book.

# Glossary of Terms

Here is a glossary of key terms used throughout the book.

1.  **Advaita Vedanta** - A non-dualistic school of Hindu philosophy that teaches the unity of the self (Atman) and the ultimate reality (Brahman).

2.  **Alchemy** - A mystical and symbolic tradition that involves the transformation of base materials into gold, often used as a metaphor for spiritual transformation.

3.  **Baqa** - In Sufism, the state of subsistence in God, where the seeker remains in constant awareness of the Divine after achieving annihilation (Fana).

4.  **Bon** - The pre-Buddhist spiritual tradition of Tibet, characterized by shamanistic and animistic practices.

5.  **Dzogchen** - A key practice in Tibetan Buddhism and Bon, focusing on realizing the primordial state of being beyond dualistic concepts.

6.  **Fana** - In Sufism, the annihilation of the self in the Divine, where the ego dissolves and the seeker experiences unity with God.

7.  **Gnosis** - A term used in Gnostic mysticism to refer to deep, experiential knowledge of the divine, leading to spiritual liberation.

8.  **Ik Onkar** - The central concept in Sikhism, meaning "One God," representing the belief in the oneness of all creation.

9.  **Kabbalah** - A mystical and esoteric tradition within Judaism, focusing on the nature of God, the universe, and the human soul.

10. **Kirtan** - A form of devotional singing in Sikhism and other spiritual traditions, used as a means of connecting with the Divine.

11. **Neidan** - Internal alchemy in Taoist mysticism, involving the cultivation of vital energies (jing, qi, shen) to achieve spiritual immortality.

12. **Pistis Sophia** - A central figure in Gnostic mysticism, representing divine wisdom and the soul's journey toward redemption.

13. **Pleroma** - In Gnostic cosmology, the fullness of the divine realm from which all spiritual beings emanate.

14. **Qi (Chi)** - In Taoism, the vital energy that flows through all living things, essential for health, vitality, and spiritual well-being.

15. **Shamanism** - An ancient spiritual tradition involving communication with the spirit world through rituals, journeying, and the use of sacred objects.

16. **Sophia** - The personification of divine wisdom in Gnostic and other mystical traditions, often associated with the feminine aspect of the Divine.

17. **Tao** - The fundamental principle in Taoism, representing the natural order of the universe and the source of all existence.

18. **Tao Te Ching** - A foundational text of Taoism attributed to Laozi, offering teachings on living in harmony with the Tao.

19. **Ubuntu** - An African philosophical concept emphasizing human interconnectedness and the idea that a person is a person through others.

20. **Wu Wei** - A Taoist concept meaning "effortless action" or "non-action," where one acts in perfect harmony with the natural order.

21. **Yin and Yang** - In Taoism, the complementary forces that represent the dualities inherent in the universe, such as light and dark, male and female.

22. **Ziran** - A Taoist concept often translated as "naturalness" or "spontaneity," referring to acting in accordance with one's true nature.

23. **Zohar** - A key text in Kabbalistic mysticism, exploring the mystical dimensions of the Torah and the nature of God.

24. **Zhuangzi** - A foundational text of Taoist philosophy attributed to Zhuang Zhou, exploring themes of naturalness, spontaneity, and the limits of human knowledge.

25. **Dreamtime** - The spiritual belief system of the Australian Aboriginal peoples, focusing on the creation myths and the interconnectedness of all beings.

www.ingramcontent.com/pod-product-compliance
Lightning Source LLC
Chambersburg PA
CBHW050649160426
43194CB00010B/1866